BETTY JANE WYLIE

solo chef¹

¹ ELLIPTICAL FOR **CHEF DE CUISINE**, MEANING YOU'RE THE HEAD HONCHO IN YOUR KITCHEN.

MACMILLAN CANADA
Toronto, Canada

Canadian Cataloguing in Publication Data

Wylie, Betty Jane, date.
   Solo chef : recipes, tips, advice and encouragement for single cooks

Includes index.
ISBN 0–7715–7396–0

1. Cookery for one.   I. Title.
TX652.W85   1997   641.5'61   C96–930955–4

1 2 3 4 5 TG 01 00 99 98 97

Cover design by Stray Toaster: Valerie Sippel
Interior design by Stray Toaster

This book is available at special discounts for bulk purchases by your group or organization for sales promotions, premiums, fundraising and seminars. For details, contact: Macmillan Canada, Special Sales Department, 29 Birch Avenue, Toronto, ON M4V 1E2. Tel: 416-963-8830.

Macmillan Canada wishes to thank the Canada Council, the Ontario Ministry of Culture and Communications and the Ontario Arts Council for supporting its publishing program.

Macmillan Canada
A Division of Canada Publishing Corporation
Toronto, Ontario, Canada

Printed in Canada

Contents

To Sherrill Harrison,
a solo chef *par excellence*

CHAPTER ONE

The Singular Facts of Life

It is a bare-footed fact that cooking and eating alone can be remarkably relaxing.

~ Peg Bracken

*E*ating is one of the few things people do by themselves that they can talk about in mixed company. A lingering Puritan ethic suggests that solitary dining is not something anyone should enjoy, but that's not borne out by the freewheeling single cooks I meet in the gourmet delis and greengrocers after the sun goes down. Forget hermits with their spring water and raw greens; disregard anchorites with their vows of silence, chastity and abstinence. Those are stereotypes that no longer attach to a person who lives alone. Whatever goes on behind your closed doors, you singles are having a good time.

Reluctant to admit their pleasure, most of the singles I have interviewed take on a crafty expression

1 MIND YOU, IT MAY NOT ALWAYS BE GOOD FOR THEM. (I COULD HAVE SAID THIS IN A PARENTHESIS, BUT I WANT YOU TO GET USED TO ASIDES.)

2 NOT HAVING TO PICK UP AFTER SOMEONE ELSE; NOT HAVING TO EXPLAIN WHERE YOU'VE BEEN IF YOU'RE LATE; NO ONE NAGGING YOU FOR AN E.T.A. OF DINNER, IN FACT NO HURRY ABOUT MEALS— OR CLEANING, FOR THAT MATTER; NO PROBLEM ABOUT CUTTING AN ARTICLE OUT OF THE NEWSPAPER BEFORE ANYONE ELSE HAS READ IT, OR WATCHING THE LATE LATE MOVIE, OR EATING IN BED. NO ONE IN BED—YOU CAN SPRAWL IF YOU WANT TO. A GOOD RELATIONSHIP, OF COURSE, BOTH TAKES AND ALLOWS FOR THESE LUXURIOUS NEGATIVES.

when I ask them to describe their singular eating habits. It's not shame but guilt they are trying to mask, because most of the time they're eating exactly what they please[1] and don't like to call too much attention to themselves. Most married civilians seem to consider munching solo in the same bracket as drinking alone: a sign of failure or an indication of decadence, and certainly a nasty habit. I think couples have to reassure themselves with this myth because they can't help noticing that singles have a remarkable capacity for self-indulgence.

Many of the advantages of the single life are defined in terms of negatives.[2] When it comes to food, however, the joys are mostly positive. When you eat alone you are free to eat all the strawberries, all the spring asparagus and all the soft centres. You can pig out on your favourite food and you can also skip a meal if you're not hungry. No one else in your care is expecting to be fed, unless you have a pet.

Not that you don't have obstacles to overcome, but most of your food skirmishes take place in the market, not the kitchen. Price Club was not invented for you. Big bags of potatoes, flour and sugar and large economy boxes, cans and tubes of anything go bad, mouldy or irrelevant before you can finish them. Even one small acorn squash presents a challenge. Big meat, that is, roasts and large birds, is impossible for a single to tackle armed with only one mouth. But there are delectable solutions to the problems faced by those who cook and eat by themselves.

Mind you, some singles are better trained to create these solutions than others—more prepared to handle solo cooking. Older ones, whether single all their lives or not, more frequently female if past a certain age, generally have a better than nodding acquaintance with a skillet and a spoon. A kitchen has figured in their lives at some time or other and they find themselves, if anything, over-equipped. But while a background in cooking may help, it may also close their minds to new methods, new products and new taste sensations.

Most older single men still like to have someone to cook for them. I used to date one older man between his marriages. He tested his third wife by allowing her to come over and cook his dinner for almost a year before they married. Before that, his usual single-boy's-night-at-home dinner was a big bowl of Shreddies smothered with brown sugar and drowned in heavy cream. It's a good thing he married again. Other men, less demanding and more adventurous, extend their skills from the backyard barbecue to the kitchen range and learn to boil water — and eggs — among other things.[3]

Many younger singles are still on the fast-food take-out circuit and will never own a cookbook like this one unless their mother gives it to them. But the increasing number of people in the median age range, both male and female, those whom divorce or other circumstances have left alone in the kitchen, means that there are a lot of you out there, with assorted tastes, incomes, culinary skills, digestions and teeth. You all face the challenge of preparing and eating your daily bread alone. The younger among you are still working; the retired usually have more time than money, and maybe a tad less energy — more patience, though.

The questions facing any single entering the kitchen are the same six that every reporter must ask and answer: who, where, when, what, how and

3 THESE DAYS NO ONE SEEMS TO KNOW HOW TO CODDLE AN EGG. I'M GOING TO TELL YOU RIGHT NOW: GENTLY DROP AN EGG INTO BOILING WATER AND LEAVE IT THERE FOR 2 MINUTES, TOPS. YOU HAVE NOW PRESUMABLY KILLED THE SALMONELLA BUT STILL HAVE A NICE OOZY TEXTURE TO PLAY WITH.

4 WE ALL KNOW ABOUT THE
BOTHER: PLANNING, SHOPPING,
PREPARING AND CLEANING UP.
AIN'T NO ONE ELSE GONNA DO IT
IF YOU DON'T.

5 FOR OTHER OCCASIONAL WHOS,
SEE CHAPTER 9.

6 I'VE BEEN TOLD THAT WHEN
WORKING SINGLES DO THAT, THEY
FALL ASLEEP WHILE THE FOOD IS
COOKING AND SPOIL EVERY-
THING—THEIR APPETITE AS
WELL AS DINNER.

why bother?[4] Who, of course, is you, most of the time.[5] Where and when are matters of lifestyle. What and how are what this book is all about. It's the *why bother?* that must be dealt with immediately.

The reason you should bother to cook well and deliciously for yourself is that you are worth it. You deserve it. All those New Age pep talks are never so apt and necessary as they are in the kitchen. If you have trouble acknowledging them, then you must begin to alter your opinion of your own worth—and your right to gourmet popcorn.

We all have to learn the art of nurturing as it pertains to eating well. Nurturing is a skill women in the past developed in relation to others, not to themselves. Nurturing is a gift men have been pleased to accept from women. Now the time has come for both sexes to nurture themselves, starting in the kitchen. A synonym for nurture is nourish, and that's what this book is about: nourishment for one.

At least part of the answer to "why bother?" is to make sure it's not much bother. You're not alone in your reluctance to dally in the kitchen. The attention span and patience of consumers in general have diminished. Whereas people used to be willing to take up to half an hour preparing a meal, they now want that time cut in half. That was my original guideline, that nothing was going to take you longer than 15 minutes to prepare. Sometimes it would take a little longer to cook, so it would help if you had a microwave oven, but you can have a drink or watch TV or read a book until the food is ready.[6] But I was wrong. Average preparation time should be closer to five minutes.

My friend Richard Teleky points out that five minutes is four minutes longer than it takes to phone take-out. Carrie Snow writes that she prefers

Hostess fruit pies to pop-up toaster tarts because they don't require so much cooking. The point is that although take-out is easy, cooking and eating for one needn't be limited to that kind of (expensive) fast food, because my recipes are going to be very fast. Neither should it be daunting for people who hate to cook, or are too busy, or who can't be bothered when there isn't a crowd to cook for. It's no bother, you see, and you have to eat.

We're up against what I call the Aristotelian Unities of the Kitchen. Just as Aristotle set down artistic rules for play construction, so must we establish Domestic Rules according to the needs and tolerance level of a singular cook.

The Singles' Canon

- ° preparation time 15 minutes max, 5 minutes better

- ° no oven (microwave or toaster-oven is okay)

- ° good taste

- ° good nutrition

- ° and low cost (except for treats)

I've done my best to stay within these guidelines, but you must know some of my basic assumptions.

Wylie's Guidelines

- ° It pays to cook ahead.[7]

- ° Sometimes Price Club is a good idea.

- ° "Optional" means I don't like it, but you might.

7 OTHERWISE, YOU'RE COOKING EVERY SINGLE NIGHT.

- Life isn't *cordon bleu* all the way.

- Appetites cannot be measured.

- Read the small print.

- Good ideas bear repeating.

- Men may cook but they forget vegetables.

- Eat your mistakes—or not.

Bothering isn't as much bother as it used to be, with all the hi-tech equipment and decent precooked packaged shortcuts on the market now. Manufacturers are even aware that people like to add their own little touches to their product, so they allow for "doctoring," even encourage it. You're already spending so much time reading in the supermarket, you might as well take an extra minute to check out the serving suggestions or the *recipe inside*—a sneaky way to make you buy the product and take it home.

Now for a few practical asides. I know we're all supposed to be thinking metric now but some habits die hard. In the case of older cooks, you'll be like me after all these years: able to measure with your eye. In fact, the hardest thing about writing a cookbook is measuring my shakes, rattles and pours. So here's a helpful table. Don't skip over it; these are the terms I use in my recipes.

Wylie's Table of Measurements

1 dash, dry, equals ⅛ teaspoon, also known as 1 pinch[8]

1 dash, wet, equals ¼ teaspoon (1 mL)

8 THE *I-HATE-TO-COOK*-COOK SAYS HER THUMB-AND-TWO-FINGER PINCH IS THE EQUIVALENT OF 1/8 TSP. SHE CALLS IT PEG BRACKEN'S RULE OF THUMB AND FOREFINGER.

1 smidge equals a scant teaspoon
(5 mL)

1 splash equals a generous teaspoon
(5 mL)

1 waft equals 1 tablespoon (15 mL)

1 dollop equals 2 tablespoons (25 mL)

1 sloosh equals ½ cup (125 mL)

A sprinkle, as with cheese, equals
½ cup (125 mL)

To dot, as with butter, equals 1 to
2 tablespoons (15 to 25 mL)

As for serving sizes, I've combined a couple of little charts, one courtesy of the Dairy Bureau of Canada, originated by Jane Kirby, RD of *Glamour* magazine, and one courtesy of *Health* magazine to give you some idea of how much you should be eating.

A thumb equals 1 ounce (25 g) of
most cheeses

A portion of cheese (as noted in
Canada's Food Guide) is about the size
of a pair of dice

A thumb-tip equals a teaspoon (5 mL)

3 thumb-tips equal a tablespoon
(15 mL)

A palm (that's without fingers and
thumb) equals a serving of cooked
meat, fish or poultry (the size of a tape
cassette if that's easier to picture)

8

A fist equals a cup (250 mL)—this is also one portion of cooked pasta or rice

One small fistful is a portion of French fries, potato chips, nuts

One portion of salad is about the size of a baseball

You're in luck if you have big hands.

A major problem for singles is how to use up prepared food before they go squirrelly and it goes green. Peg Bracken suggests that the solution to this problem is to "buy only what you truly like, and eat all of it at once." Obviously, eating all the soup in the can or the whole box of Kraft dinner in one sitting is no way to deal with an overage of food, neither cost-effective nor healthy—also, it means you have to cook again. Irma Rombauer, she of *The Joy of Cooking*, defined eternity as "two people and a ham." When there's just one of you even a cauliflower feels like forever. There's no point in buying and cooking all this food if you're just going to end up throwing it out. These days no one can afford to do that. I have developed a philosophy of leftovers; it's called being frugal.

It's said that variety is the spice of life; singles just have to take their variety in more concentrated doses. You have to develop a short but intensely focused attention to food and cultivate longer-range eating habits. If you have purchased at great expense a tiny basket of fresh raspberries, you are going to eat them all, aren't you? What you don't finish for dessert you sprinkle on a bowl of cereal in the morning. Like that. You're just going to have to eat more of a smaller number of things in a given time period. Some things you won't mind, like those delectable raspberries. Others will bore you.

A good way to be sure to use up stuff is to shop for related foods, items that will go with the major purchase: a peach to make a Melba with the last of your raspberries; (light) cream cheese to extend the last morsel of smoked salmon; Parmesan cheese to sprinkle on the leftover cooked asparagus (on toast).

FRUGAL IS AS FRUGAL DOES

> *A chicken doesn't stop scratching just because the worms are scarce.*
>
> ~ *Grandma Soderquist's Conclusion*

The late American money expert Sylvia Porter estimated that it costs 20 per cent more to feed one person alone than to feed one person in a family of four. As with other areas of a single's budget, there are not many expenses that can be realistically reduced. It costs as much to heat one body in a room as two. Fixed costs are just that—fixed—not to say rising these days, including the price of food. It always has been hard to make ends meet, but it gets harder as the ends spread farther apart; the temptation is to make all the cutbacks in food costs. So we'll do some serious thinking here, while never letting go of our intention to enjoy good food.

When I was making my way as a journalist, I left home once and went to live on Old Age Security, the amount of money a single 65-year-old without any other means of support had to live on. I did it on assignment for the *Toronto Star*. When I suggested it to the editor, he jumped at the idea, with one condition: "Wait until it's colder," he said. "I want you to suffer."

I learned a lot from my Old Lady Caper, as I dubbed it. It was my introduction to living completely on my own. I found a room in a rooming house in the east end of the city where I shared a bathroom and a fridge in the upstairs hall with three men who drank a lot of beer, thus defining the use of both facilities. From that room and that perspective I began to explore. I found an Elderly Persons Centre that ran a co-op store on Thursday afternoons and Friday mornings where I could buy potatoes by the one; I found a day-old bread store; I went to a women's hostel on Sunday nights for dinner, and for the vegetables and conversation. I learned later that after my series was published in the *Star*, entire classes in community colleges were assigned my grocery list, which I had included, and told to cook a balanced menu of meals from my ingredients.

Though my intent was to do the research necessary to write a play about an old woman in a room,[9] I learned a few pragmatic lessons from the experience, including the importance of, for example, a stock pot, fresh garlic, chocolate and patience.

I already knew a fair bit about frugality and nutrition from rearing four children both with and without a husband; I acquired more in the three weeks I spent juggling that tiny amount of money and adjusting to living alone on a tight budget, and I'll share some of my tips with you. I'm going to tell you some things your mother didn't tell you, mainly because she didn't know them either.[10]

Too many skills and tricks have been neglected and forgotten. This is one of the advantages of being my age: I know a few secrets, and no one has burned me at the stake yet so I can still pass on my lore.

Stay with me.

9 MY MOST PRODUCED PLAY. *A PLACE ON EARTH* HAS BEEN PERFORMED IN NEW ZEALAND, GREAT BRITAIN AND THE UNITED STATES AS WELL AS CANADA. OLD WOMEN IN ROOMS ARE TO BE FOUND ALL OVER THE WORLD.

10 I'M PROBABLY OLDER THAN SHE IS, TOO.

CHAPTER TWO

Lifestyle

Tell me what you eat, and I will tell you what you are.

~ *Brillat-Savarin*
Physiologie du Goût, 1825

Singles' eating habits are fascinating, not just what they eat, but where and when. *Where* is first: location, location, location. I conducted an informal survey to find out where singles eat. The majority of you dine in a chair in front of the TV with a favourite newscaster to tell you about the day that was. Some use a TV table, some a tray, some a side table, some a beanbag laptop. Most use a fork, seldom a knife; about half use a napkin, usually paper; some use a sheet of paper towelling, others a tea towel instead of a place mat.[1]

In spite of the need to keep informed, most singles have several alternative eating venues away from the television. Sometimes the food dictates a

1 FINGER FOOD IS A NATURAL FOR SINGLES, WITH THEIR AVERSION TO WASHING DISHES, THEIR CHANGING VENUES FOR EATING AND THEIR TENDENCY TO EAT ON THE RUN. I'VE BEEN THINKING A LOT ABOUT THE THINGS YOU CAN PUT ON, IN, ON TOP OF, UNDER OR AROUND FOOD TO MAKE IT FINGERABLE. SO, JUST FOR YOU NOSHERS, AND FOR OTHERS WHO CAN'T STAND WASHING DISHES, I WILL INSERT FINGER FOODS IN AMONGST THE RECIPES.

more stable surface, hence the kitchen table. I know lots of people who eat a bowl of cereal[2] or maybe a bowl of pasta at the corner of the kitchen table. Fettuccine is a bit sloppy to eat in an armchair, but it depends on the consistency and colour of the sauce and how washable your chair is. One single woman told me she usually eats lunch standing at the kitchen sink looking out the window at the birds.[3] In good weather, a lot of solitary diners take to a porch or deck or balcony, or failing that, an open window with a view. I live on a lake. When the sun is irresistible, I carry a picnic lunch in a basket to my dock. In bad weather, or in a blue funk, also known as depression, many singles take a tray to bed and stay there, often with the bedroom television turned on or with a book. I don't have a bed with a headboard to lean on because I sleep on a futon; my solution is my big ugly recliner chair and popcorn.

It seems impossible to discuss the *where* without falling into the *what*, and it's true, the choice of food often dictates the venue for consuming it, and vice versa, and some things taste better depending on where you eat them: hot dogs at a ball game, cotton candy at a midway, popcorn at the movies,[4] sandwiches on a picnic, hamburgers at a drive-in, chestnuts while you're roasting by an open fire. Still, the food you consume and the place you choose to consume it is your choice, as capricious as your appetite.

Movable feasts are not restricted to dates or dinner time in a single's household. I knew a widow who used to prepare a breakfast tray to enjoy in bed on mornings when there was a classic movie she wanted to watch on television. Lots of people, singles included, tuck an apple and a hunk of cheese in their fanny packs when they go for a walk and pause for a picnic in a park. The point is not to feel you're chained to a table or a rut. Anywhere that suits your fancy is okay, so long as it's safe [5]

I do understand that some singles feel lonely if they do it at a table. Me too, but I know one person who always sets a proper table, lights a candle and eats her meal in solitary splendour. The awesome result is that she is slim. Diet experts will tell you that you shouldn't do anything else but eat when you eat. Take a bite, put your fork down between bites, chew, think beautiful thoughts, eat, but don't do anything else. I think the idea is that you get so bored you want to get it over with, so you don't eat much. Bad thinking. No one really eats alone at a table.[6]

The point is that no one sits at a table and does nothing but eat. Listen, if you were eating with someone, you wouldn't do it in silence, unless you were having a fight. (So you wouldn't be just not talking then, you'd be ruining your digestion.) There is no reason to sit in utter uninformed silence when you eat alone, no reason to feel you have to defend your choice of supplementary activity, and no reason not to eat wherever you choose, including in bed. There are worse things people do in bed.

When you eat is as open an option as where for singles, but if you have a job, timing can be a problem. Most working singles I interviewed tend to skip breakfast entirely or wait until they get to the office and coffee break. Not great for the blood sugar level. A significant proportion of these busy people go on to skip lunch. Then their evening meal begins about six and continues until bedtime. Thus the bulk of

5 *TAKE THE BATHROOM OFF YOUR LIST. A LOT OF WOMEN BREAKFAST IN THE BATHROOM AS THEY CURL, MOUSSE OR STEAM THEIR HAIR. TAKE A BITE, TWIST THAT CURL, TAKE A BITE, FLICK THAT COMB. NOT MANY MEN TRY TO EAT WHILE THEY SHAVE BECAUSE SHAVING CREAM DOESN'T TASTE GOOD. I'M A GREAT BELIEVER IN "AS-YOU" ACTIVITY—DOING SOMETHING ELSE AS YOU DO SOMETHING—BUT THIS IS CARRYING EFFICIENCY TOO FAR. IT CAN'T BE GOOD FOR YOUR DIGESTION, OR YOUR DIET.*

6 *NOW PEOPLE ARE GOING TO WRITE ME AND TELL ME THEY DO. JUST TELL ME, WHAT ELSE IS AT THAT TABLE WITH YOU? A BOOK, THE PAPER, THE MAIL, A MAGAZINE, THE TV GUIDE AND THE MONITOR? THEN YOU AREN'T ALONE AT THE TABLE.*

their food intake for the day settles in their sedentary bodies for the night. They are not alone.[7] People will tell you—they tell me—that they simply can't eat when they first get up, that they have to warm up, take their time—which they don't have. A slow basal metabolism is at the root of their problem, compounded by their habits. The best idea for a slow starter would be a brown bag breakfast.

Unemployed and retired singles, young and old, cannot claim the pressures of the work day as their excuse for either fasting or bingeing at breakfast. Lack of money, lack of energy or interest, lack of self-esteem or simply boredom can all contribute to a breakfast boycott, no matter where it isn't consumed. Let's just say that breakfast presents a challenge, one that I hope to meet.

Lunch, too, varies according to the day and the occupation of the single consumer, and I will try to take that into account. Dinner, of course, is inexorable, and brings us face to face with a world of demographics. Time of life, time available, the money and energy at our disposal and shifting circumstances all contribute to our eating habits, and change them, subtly or not so, according to the variables.

When I was first married and learning to cook (My Other Life), I stumbled on casseroles, the "in" thing in the 1950s. They suited me very well because I didn't have a dining room. My coffee table pulled up and drop leaves spread their wings to make a dining table for four, but I had to serve dinner guests numbering more than two on television tables. Therefore I did not serve big meat because it was hard to cut on a wobbly table. I specialized in casseroles, producing every recipe in a *Good Housekeeping* special pull-out section, and also in Marion

Tracy's two books about casserole cooking, long since out of print. Amazing combinations appeared in my attractive oven-to-table dishes, complete with stands and warmer candles. A casserole, salad and interesting bread, beginning but not ending with garlicked French, made up my meals. Casseroles were interesting and charming, and so, I thought, was I.[8]

In a while, when I had a baby, I used to cook in the morning, making a casserole that I would pop into the oven when I sat down in the late afternoon to nurse the baby before putting her to sleep. Very efficient. Also economical. The only trouble with casseroles is that they usually feed six. For you, I'm going to talk about cooking less than that.

There's another food habit everyone carries around like a post-hypnotic command, and that's an addiction to comfort food.

8 WE ALL LIVE ON THE PEAKS OF PLATITUDES, TAKING NOTHING BUT SHORT VIEWS.

COMFORT FOOD

I have always maintained that there is nothing wrong with nursery food now that we are grown up and can have a glass of wine with it.

~ Elizabeth Ray

The food of our early childhood holds a terrific power over our eating habits, no matter how old or young we are. As writer-cook Laurie Colwin points out, "when people enter the kitchen they often drag their childhood with them." I have a very fastidious friend, a genuine soft-boiled-egg lady, who has never been adventurous in her eating habits. Yet every once in a while, to her husband's horror, she brings home a hunk of blood sausage and eats slabs of it on dark bread, smiling all the while. Her Scottish father used to give it to her when she was a child and she has loved it ever since.

I used to eat hardfish from my Icelandic grand-mother's back shed in Gimli, Manitoba — whole split boned fish that had been spread out in the sun to dry thus preserving it for the winter in those days before freezers. Tough and salty, it was best ripped off in a chunk that was used as a shovel to dig up soft butter to eat it with. As an adult I offered it to my husband, claiming it as one of my early childhood treats. He refused it, saying it tasted like dried toenails.[9]

Before I had a vegetable steamer, but after my daughter Liz was grown and out of the parental home, she came over for dinner one evening and I burned the cauliflower. She was ecstatic. "Burned cauliflower!" she raved. "I haven't had that for years."

She was the first child of four. I used to turn on the food as I nursed the baby before bedtime. Often I was too slow and burned the veg. To Liz burned cauliflower became a symbol of home and family and all being right with the world.

I am trying to show you with these stories the kind of magic we invest in food and its power to comfort us. I am fully aware of how intimate per-sonal food foibles are and how impossible it is to suggest anyone's favourite comfort food.

Nevertheless.

It makes interesting reading, I think, and who knows? You may discover a new comfort food, some-thing in your personal chemistry that was missing and you never knew it until now. That's how I felt about pesto, which I didn't discover until I was 43.

9 I WANTED TO KNOW HOW HE KNEW WHAT DRIED TOENAILS TASTED LIKE.

The late writer-cook M.F.K. Fisher commented that almost every person has something secret he likes to eat, and I think that's true.[10] I know several people who simply love toast. It has to be the right colour, texture and heat, and it has to be spread with butter soft enough to ooze right in and it should be cut in triangles, never horizontally. And if they were to have a perfectly soft-boiled egg with it, they would be very, very comforted. Very nursery.

I've already mentioned two of the major taste sensations of comfort food: chocolate and bread. Eggs are another, and not only soft-boiled. Put them together with chocolate and bread and comfort a lot of people.

10 *I'LL CONFESS ONE, WHICH I GAVE UP, BECAUSE IT'S TOO DECADENT. IT'S AN EASY FIX FOR A SINGLE WHO CRAVES CHOCOLATE. I USED TO KEEP A TIN OF CHOCOLATE FROSTING IN THE FREEZER ALONG WITH A BAG OF WHOLE PECANS. ONE PECAN USED AS A CHIP TO DIP UP A LITTLE CHOCOLATE FROSTING IS EASIER, FASTER AND LESS EXPENSIVE THAN A BOX OF TURTLES, SO I USED TO JUSTIFY MYSELF. FINALLY I GOT TOUGH WITH MYSELF, THREW OUT THE FROSTING, AND MADE MY WALDORF SALAD WITH THE REMAINING PECANS.*

COMFORTING BREAD PUDDING

2 eggs

½ cup (125 mL) vanilla sugar

½ cup (125 mL) milk

1½ cups (375 mL) half-and-half cream

⅓ cup (75 mL) butter melted with

2 oz (56 g) of sweetened chocolate

3 or 4 half-inch-thick slices of bread, torn up (about 3 cups/750 mL)

Beat together the eggs, sugar, milk and cream, stir in the melted butter and chocolate, pour over the bread in a buttered 1-quart (1 L) oven-proof dish and let stand for 20 minutes. Bake at 350°F (180°C) for 45 minutes. To paint that lily, sift icing sugar over

the pudding before serving. Good for breakfast! This will serve more than one, but go ahead and pig out.

Some people think comfort food is nursery food, and it can be, but not always. The feeling goes back to childhood, swift memory flashes of moments of pleasure, often related to food and drink: hot soup for lunch on a cold day; cold lemonade on a hot afternoon; egg and onion sandwiches on a picnic; leftover-turkey sandwiches with lots of hot gravy; corn on the cob at a corn roast; hot cocoa frothed with marshmallows after a sleigh ride; a perfect soft-boiled egg with toast fingers for the first day of food after the flu; chocolate pudding like mother used to make — by this time you should be off on a memory trip of your own.

We chew on memory when we eat comfort food. Of course, we also derive sustenance and often strength from the food itself. It has been said that left to itself, the body knows what it needs.[11] I remember when I was incubating an ulcer, bleeding internally before I knew it, I had this fierce craving for liver. I was in New York with my husband and at every divine restaurant we went to, I ordered liver. I was as surprised as he was, but it may have been what kept me from bleeding to death before I got home for blood transfusions. Just bear in mind that when your mind craves comfort, it may be your body demanding something, stomach's ease as well as heart's.

People have always given food credit for its therapeutic qualities: hot lemon and honey, with or without rum, for a cold; milk toast and beef tea for invalids; chicken soup for just about anything: "It won't hurt and it might help." Vitamins have added to the mystique, the ones lurking there in the food and the expensive bottled ones that promise us, if not immortality, at least a long and healthy life.

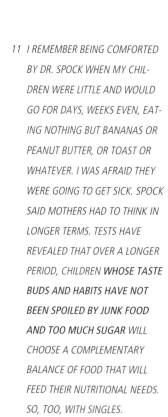

*11 I REMEMBER BEING COMFORTED BY DR. SPOCK WHEN MY CHILDREN WERE LITTLE AND WOULD GO FOR DAYS, WEEKS EVEN, EATING NOTHING BUT BANANAS OR PEANUT BUTTER, OR TOAST OR WHATEVER. I WAS AFRAID THEY WERE GOING TO GET SICK. SPOCK SAID MOTHERS HAD TO THINK IN LONGER TERMS. TESTS HAVE REVEALED THAT OVER A LONGER PERIOD, CHILDREN **WHOSE TASTE BUDS AND HABITS HAVE NOT BEEN SPOILED BY JUNK FOOD AND TOO MUCH SUGAR** WILL CHOOSE A COMPLEMENTARY BALANCE OF FOOD THAT WILL FEED THEIR NUTRITIONAL NEEDS. SO, TOO, WITH SINGLES.*

Comfort doesn't have to come in soft packages. Crisp is good, too. You've heard expressions like "it sticks in my craw," "spit it out," "chewing out" someone you're mad at and "chewing nails" when you're really angry. These food images give us an indication of another kind of comfort to be derived from food. Texture. Crunch. Resistance, because sometimes it makes you feel good when food fights back.[12] No one's going to get angry with you if you tear food to pieces in the privacy of your home.

If you've had a rough day and you feel like fighting back, buy a whole (small) barbecued chicken at the deli counter, take it home and tear it apart with your bare hands, rip it to shreds with your teeth, and eat it ferociously. Pull crusty muesli bread into big chunks and cram them into your mouth and chew them viciously. Oh, for heaven's sake, chomp on a celery stick if you can't find anything else.

Nuts are good, and you could spike them. Toss peanuts in chili powder and roast them 10 to 12 minutes in a 350°F (180°C) oven, stirring or shaking a few times so they won't burn. Try cashews with curry, almonds with soy sauce.

If you like sweet nuts to chew on, do this:

12 FOOD PURVEYORS CONSIDER "MOUTH-FEEL" AN IMPORTANT SELLING POINT IN ANY FOOD.

COMFORTING SPICED NUTS

1 cup (250 mL) sugar

1 tsp (5 mL) ground cardamom

⅛ tsp (pinch) nutmeg

½ cup (125 mL) evaporated milk

1 tbsp (15 mL) water

3 cups (750 mL) mixed nuts, your choice but no peanuts

13 IN MY OTHER LIFE I USED TO MAKE BREAD WHEN I WAS UPSET. NOT ONLY THEN, OF COURSE, BUT WHEN SOMETHING BAD WAS GOING ON, LIKE WHEN MY FATHER WAS DYING, OR WHEN I WAS IMPOTENTLY ANGRY. CAUGHT IN A SITUATION I COULD DO NOTHING ABOUT, I MADE BREAD. KNEADING AND POUND-ING DOUGH IS ONE OF THE SAFEST OUTLETS YOU CAN FIND FOR YOUR ANGER, AND IT'S PRODUC-TIVE, TOO. SINGLES DON'T HAVE MUCH TIME FOR BREAD BAKING, NOT THE OLD, SLOW-RISING WAY, AND THE NEW FAST-RISING YEAST ELIMINATES KNEADING. STILL, YOU MUST BE ABLE TO FIND SOME-THING SAFE TO PUNCH AROUND. BISQUICK WILL DO. IF YOU MAKE UP A SHORTCAKE OR BISCUITS ACCORDING TO PACKAGE DIREC-TIONS, YOU SHOULD BE ABLE TO SLAP THE DOUGH AROUND BEFORE YOU SHAPE IT.

14 NOTHING IS EVER SIMPLE.

Combine everything but the nuts in a saucepan and bring to a boil—to the soft ball stage (236°F/113°C on a candy thermometer)—and never stop stirring. Take the mixture off the heat, dump in the nuts, and stir until the spoon stops. Turn the stuff out onto waxed paper or foil and let it cool. When you and they are cool enough, separate the clump into chew-able pieces. Chew.

Why do you think singles like popcorn and rice cakes so much? Not just because they're low-fat. Because they're crunchy, and you can chew, munch, chomp, gnaw, masticate, mash, grind and pulverize them with your teeth. All very good ways to release anger.

But this is still taking it out on yourself, that is, on your body. You may have taught that popcorn a les-son or made sure that those (low-fat) pretzels will never make trouble for you again, but what else have you done? Added more calories to your load. Rather than all that vicious chewing, why don't you try slapping something around?[13]

Cracking nuts from their shell might help—even peanuts? If you do a lot of them you could make peanut soup, but then you'd have to have someone for dinner.[14] Or you could freeze it.

My advice is to take comfort wherever you find it, and I'll keep offering it. In the kitchen, that is. It's still the safest place to go wild.

COOKING METHODS

A recipe for fish baked in ashes:
No cheese, no nonsense! Just place it tenderly in fig leaves and tie them on top with a string; then push it under hot ashes, bethinking thee wisely of the time when it is done, and burn it not up.

~ Archestratus, 4th century B.C.

Cooking methods have as much to do with habits and lifestyle as anything else that goes on in the kitchen. I think method cooking is like method acting: it depends on your motivation. We all think we know the basics of cooking, even if we don't do it. After all, we've been eating mostly cooked food all our lives; we must be aware of how it mutates from field or factory to kitchen and table.

Heat. You need heat to change the texture and edibility of most food. Most of the world cooks over fire, without many utensils. (It's species memory that drives men to barbecue.) But how do you handle the heat? Here's what most cooks do and what it means to us and to the food:

° **boil:** to cook in boiling water

° **poach:** to cook gently in simmering (usually) water

° **fry:** to cook in shallow fat or oil, also called sauté

° **deep-fry:** to cook in deep fat (like French-fried potatoes)

° **soupée:**[15] to sauté in a frozen soup cube

15 *I MADE UP THIS WORD. MEMORIZE IT BECAUSE I USE IT A LOT.*

- **braise:** to brown in fat and cook in liquid

- **bake:** to cook in an oven, as bread, cake, cookies

- **roast:** to cook using dry heat, as in an oven

- **broil:** to cook over or under direct heat, electric, gas or fire,

also called

- **grill:** very English

- **steam:** to cook over boiling water

- **zap (or nuke):** to cook, warm, or reconcile food in a microwave

Obviously, some of these methods have to go because you have no time to braise and you should go easy on the fat. But steaming and zapping make up for a lot of braising and broasting.[16] Broiling, grilling, barbecueing are all fast and fun.

I think this is a good time to reconsider Girl Guide Cooking. In my old Girl Guide camping days, everyone was given a piece of foil—yes, they had foil then—a hunk of meat and chunks of onion, carrot and potato, plus a go at the salt and pepper. Everyone wrapped her own dinner and found a place for it in the hot coals of a campfire. After a suitable time spent singing, the packages were fished out and the contents devoured. It wasn't great food but it's a great memory. I mentioned this to my granddaughter Meg, and this method turns out to have filtered down to her generation. She was very

16 *A METHOD EVOLVED BY MANUFACTURERS WHO HAVE DEVELOPED A METHOD AND AN APPLIANCE THAT DEEP-FRIES IN A CLOSED UNIT.*

knowledgeable and a great help, being familiar with this kind of cookout stuff on camping trips with her other custodial parent. She told me what they put in their foil packages now, mostly vegetables. The point is, these are *individual* servings.

You can't put metal in a microwave, so I bought parchment paper—also known as baking paper—and proceeded to wrap things to see how they turned out. The first package, filled according to memory, was terrible. Chunks of stewing beef have no chance to get tender in 4 minutes in a micro-wave. But I went on from there. There was one out-standing quick dinner, using a pork chop; you'll find it on p. 178. I tried a variety of vegetable packages and a pillow of banana, rum and brown sugar that was just too decadent to record.

The most rewarding aspect of these packages is the speed. Cooking in parchment is a time-hon-oured method with a beautiful name in French—*en papillote*—a method reserved for delicate food, like veal or fish. The paper is cut in the shape of a heart, oiled or buttered, and wrapped around the food or fish. I am not so dainty. I wrap my parcels with a generous drugstore wrap, fold the ends under and vent each side with several knife stabs. No butter, no fat, just enough moisture[17] to keep the food from drying out. I suppose it steams, really. Anyway, it works. You saw it here first.

It takes time and attention to eat well and fru-gally, dragging your memories and your habits with you. Habits are hard to break. This is an opportunity for you to assess yours and decide what, if anything, to do about them. You may be happily set in your ways. You may be searching for a challenge. The kitchen is a pretty safe place to start looking.

17 *A DASH OF BOTTLED SAUCE, A FROZEN SOUP CUBE OR A FEW DROPS OF LEMON JUICE, DEPENDING ON THE FOOD AND YOUR TASTE BUDS.*

EQUIPMENT, A DISCUSSION

What sort of person is it who doesn't own a food mill?

~ Laurie Colwin

While you're looking for challenges, take time to analyze your equipment. In My Other Life, I owned too much, not only in the kitchen. My culinary equipment was symptomatic of a consumer attitude. I had everything from individual cornucopia tins to an oyster shucker to a mushroom brush. I still have a couscousière, though with the new instant couscous mixes I haven't used it for a while. Sometimes I use my lemon zester.

I mention this at the outset because some single cooks are like me: downsizing and loving it. I refer to My Other Life in capitals because I am no longer that person who owned all that stuff and who fussed so much.[18] Others, more fortunate in a way, are just beginning to get a grip on their lives and their possessions and thinking twice before they make any major purchases. Perhaps I can help you not to make the mistakes I made so that you will be free to make others.

You don't really need much to function in a kitchen. A skillet, a knife, a spoon, a can-opener and a corkscrew could just about do it, although when I did my Old Lady Caper, I took along my stock pot, good for soup as well as pasta. It's pretty hard to strain pasta without a colander. See? One thing leads to another, and pretty soon you have a kitchen full of equipment.

My basic list of essential equipment that I think a single at whatever stage needs in today's kitchen

18 *I EVEN USED TO DESCALE MY ASPARAGUS.*

begins with a microwave.[19] This is a single's necessity. It's much much more than a glorified bagel warmer or coffee heater. It's the answer to leftovers (the question being, what do I do with this?) and the secret to a single's speed and efficiency in the kitchen. I don't think you need a huge one with a control panel like the dashboard of a Lexus. Ten years ago I bought a stripped-down model with only two choices: on or off. Somewhere in between lies the answer to your cooking with both style and speed.

I tested the recipes in mine and I realize that yours is likely different. Here's a handy chart to give you some idea of how to find the balance between mine, yours and state-of-the-art microwaves. The times shown in the recipes are based on this table:[20]

Most people choose one heat (called COOK or HIGH) and leave it at that. Of course, it pays to be more subtle. Remember that the power works from

19 TO REMOVE A LINGERING ODOUR FROM YOUR MICROWAVE OVEN: SPREAD SLICES OF CUCUMBER ON A MICROWAVE DISH AND COOK ON HIGH FOR FIVE MINUTES. YOU CAN PURÉE THE COOKED CUCUMBER AND DROP IT INTO SOUP IF YOU LIKE, BUT IT DOESN'T OWE YOU A THING.

20 BEAR IN MIND THE COMMON LAW: WHEN ALL ELSE FAILS, READ THE DIRECTIONS. CONSULT YOUR OWNER'S MANUAL.

POWER LEVEL CHART[21]

Power	Output	%	Use
High	700 watts	100%	boil water, cook fruits and veg; cook fish; cook poultry; heat beverages
Medium High	650 watts	90%	heat frozen food (no eggs or cheese); heat canned food; reheat leftovers
Medium	490 watts	70%	cook meats; cook shellfish, delicate foods
Low	200 watts	30%	simmer soups; soften butter
Warm	70 watts	10%	keep foods warm
Defrost	245 watts	35%	all thawing
Delay Stand	0 watts	0%	aftercooking

21 THE STANDARDS HAVE BEEN SET BY THE INTERNATIONAL MICROWAVE POWER INSTITUTE, WHICH SOUNDS AS IF IT COULD TAKE OVER THE WORLD.

the outside in so put the slower-cooking food, the thickest cuts, or the longest-cooking vegetables around the perimeter of your cooking dish, circling the tender items like mushrooms or peppers or fish in the centre. Pay attention, too, to the effectiveness of aftercooking—a kind of resting period while the zapped food gets acclimatized. You don't have to leave the food in the microwave; take it out and drape it with foil, over an open casserole, or a hand towel over a covered dish. Perhaps a little undercooked when you take it out, the food will continue to cook for one or two minutes *on the last power level*[22] after you take it out. Anyway, your goal is the same as it always was. It's called "cook until done."

Some people, especially older ones, tell me they couldn't live without their toaster-oven, and it's true, it's almost as useful as the microwave, especially if you still eat a lot of meat. This appliance can be used for broiling one or two hamburgers, a small steak, a couple of chicken breasts, a piece of liver (it's good for you) or anything with cheese on top that requires melting. The value of a toaster-oven is twofold: it doesn't use as much power as the oven broiler and it's easier to clean. I know a single woman who has managed nicely without a stove for well over a year now, thanks to her microwave and her toaster-oven.

One more appliance I consider essential is a food processor, but not a great big one; a mini-processor will do very well. I use it every day for pesto, cheese, sauces, crumbs, salad dressings, the list so endless I have difficulty thinking of it all. All I know is I wash it every day. It's easy to wash, too, and so small it doesn't take up a lot of room on the counter, a bonus since

22 *I THINK MAYBE JAMES THURBER'S GRANDMOTHER WAS ON TO SOMETHING WHEN SHE WORRIED ABOUT ELECTRICITY LEAKING OUT OF THE PLUG RECEPTACLES. I WONDER IF WE EAT MICRO-WAVED FOOD TOO SOON WHETHER THE LAST POWER LEVEL WILL START RICOCHETING AROUND INSIDE US.*

the working space of most singles tends to be small.

Before I give it all away, let's get on with the list of things I consider to be handy, if not essential.

Equipment, A List

° microwave oven

° toaster-oven

° a mini-food processor

° pop-up toaster (not necessary if your toaster-oven is automatic)[23]

° a good can-opener, electric if you're arthritic, but be sure to have a manual one for backup

° a cast-iron frying pan[24], three sizes if possible (they nest, for tighter storage) (It would be nice to have several sizes of skillets but if you have to make a choice, choose the big one to double as a wok.)

° a couple of pots, with lids, small and smaller

° a vegetable steamer, especially if you don't have a microwave

° a big stock pot, good for pasta too, and corn

° 3 good knives:
    1 paring knife
    1 8-inch (20 cm) chef's knife
    1 10-inch (25 cm) serrated slicing knife

23 LIVING AS I DO NOW IN A REGION WHERE POWER FAILURES HAPPEN WITH UNPREDICTABLE BUT CERTAIN FREQUENCY, I HAVE TO ADMIT THAT I'M ASHAMED OF MYSELF FOR PUTTING FOUR ELECTRIC APPLIANCES AT THE TOP OF MY LIST. I'M ASSUMING AN URBAN READERSHIP THAT TAKES ELECTRICITY FOR GRANTED. I DO HAVE A GRID THAT FITS THE ANDIRONS IN MY FIREPLACE AND I HAVE COOKED ON IT. AND I AM CAPABLE OF CHOPPING AND BLENDING WITH A KNIFE IF MY LITTLE PROCESSOR DIES. I DON'T EXPECT ANYONE TO DO THESE THINGS AS A REGULAR HABIT, AND I THINK WE SHOULD ALL BE GRATEFUL FOR HYDRO.

24 CAST-IRON IS BETTER THAN NON-STICK BECAUSE YOU ACTUALLY INGEST SOME OF THE IRON AND THAT'S GOOD FOR YOU

° a swivel-blade vegetable peeler

° hanging tools: metal spatula, spoon, slotted spoon, egg lifter, sharp-pronged fork, soup ladle. You can begin with a basic set and add specialty items. A set usually comes with a hanging rack, but you can arrange your own hooks anywhere you like.

° tongs—without which I cannot function

° measuring cups, measuring spoons, bowls

° 2 wooden spoons and 2 rubber spatulas and one whisk

° kettle[25]

° baking dishes—you know your needs better than I do

° roasting pan, not too large

° kitchen shears—a friend gave me a pair that fits in a sheath on the wall and I wonder what I ever did without them

25 WHISTLING OR ELECTRIC, IF YOU'RE AS ABSENT-MINDED AS I AM, BECAUSE SOMETHING EITHER HAS TO ALERT ME TO THE FACT THAT THE KETTLE IS BOILING DRY OR TO STOP ITSELF SINCE I HAVEN'T ENOUGH SENSE TO.

There is one more thing that I consider absolutely integral to my survival as a single consumer and that is a set—at least 8 (12 would be better)—of low-sided oven-to-table dishes. They are my solution to leftovers. When I cook too much, either deliberately or by accident, I freeze a good-sized serving in one of these dishes, covered with both plastic wrap and foil (to prevent the food drying out). When I'm busy doing other things or I don't feel like cooking or I'm late or whatever—when I want a quick meal—I take this dinner-in-a-dish out of the freezer, remove the foil cover and vent the plastic one and pop it in the microwave, to thaw and heat, turning or stirring the contents if necessary.

Stir used to mean to blend with a circular motion; in the microwave context, stir means to bring the hot stuff from the outside in to the cool stuff in the middle.

Sometimes, depending on the food, I will sprinkle some grated cheese on top or spread on a little salsa—nice on a frittata, for example. With or without a salad, this is a no-fuss, instant dinner at its best.

To save on dishes, consider baskets.[26] I love baskets, and it's a good thing because in the course of a year I seem to acquire a lot of them, all shapes and sizes, with and without handles. People use baskets of varying sizes in every room in the house: in the bathroom for guest soap and hotel shampoo, Q-tips and fingertip towels; in or on the desk for paper clips, Post-it notes, thumb tacks, elastic bands, stamps and oddments; in the bedroom for lipsticks, change, buttons, safety pins and key chains; in the kitchen for fruit, garlic bread, popcorn and pretzels; in the living room for magazines, catalogues, brochures and kindling; at the front door for gloves and mail. And there's still some left over. So why not use a basket to carry your food around?[27] Line it with a paper napkin, or foil, to keep your finger food warm, and go where your fancy dictates.

Here's a finger food for your basket, to get you going.

26 WHEN NOT IN USE, BASKETS TAKE UP A LOT OF SPACE IN A CUPBOARD. TREAT THEM AS PART OF THE DECOR AND ARRANGE THEM ON A KITCHEN WALL OR HANG THE ONES WITH HANDLES FROM THE CEILING IN CLUSTERS OR SINGLY. IF YOU'RE WORRIED ABOUT DUST, TAKE OFF YOUR GLASSES.

27 I BEGAN TO DO THIS YEARS AGO IN MY OTHER LIFE WHEN WE TOOK OUR VACATION AT A COTTAGE. BASKETS WERE A NATURAL ADDITION TO THE HELP-YOURSELF WAYS OF SUMMER LIVING, GIVING EVERYONE FREEDOM OF CHOICE FROM A TRAY OF SANDWICH FIXINGS, AND SAVING ON THE DISHES. INITIALLY I BOUGHT A DOZEN OR SO SMALL MATCHING BASKETS TO FEED A GROUP, BUT LATER I USED WHATEVER CAME TO HAND. PEOPLE COULD FILL THEIR BASKET WITH WHATEVER THEY WANTED AND THEY COULD BE SOCIABLE AND EAT WITH THE OTHERS OR THEY COULD PICK UP THEIR BASKET AND HIDE—ON THE RAFT IN THE SUN, ON THE DOCK IN THE SHADE, IN A HAMMOCK WITH A BOOK.

PITA EGG SALAD

> 2 hard-cooked eggs, coarsely chopped
>
> 1 frozen chicken soup cube, zapped to thaw with 1 tsp (5 mL) curry, to release the flavour
>
> 2 green onions, chopped
>
> 2 stalks celery, chopped

Chop, mix and pile into a pita pocket. (If it doesn't hang together the way you're used to, stir in a smidge of mayo.)

As for the extras—all those elegant gadgets that abound in cuisine stores—be careful. You don't *need* a garlic press; just press the clove with the flat blade of your chopping knife. You don't need stainless steel skewers for your stuffed turkey or chicken.[28] Use bamboo skewers that come in a big economy package, and then you have kebab sticks as well. I would say you do need a colander to strain your pasta. You don't need a mortar and pestle, use your mini-processor instead. You don't need a feather pastry brush—if you still make pastry that needs painting—or a baster. Buy a small paint brush at the hardware store, much cheaper. If you really need a barbecue baster, for slooshing marinade on something, use a clean squirt bottle like a detergent bottle.

The trick is to think laterally. If you don't have something, think of what you do have that will serve the purpose. You'll be pleased at your own ingenuity. As Laurie Colwin said, in her charming book *Home Cooking*, "there is no point at all in anything that only does one job." Use that comment as your

28 —IF, IN FACT, YOU EVER STUFF A TURKEY OR CHICKEN. A WHOLE PEELED ONION HELPS THE POOR BIRD NOT TO FEEL TOO EMPTY AND IT'S MUCH LOWER CALORIE THAN ALL THAT BREAD STUFF. HOWEVER, THERE ARE PEOPLE WHO WOULD KILL FOR STUFFING, AND IF YOU'RE ONE OF THEM, JUST IGNORE ME.

caution before you start accumulating too much and also when you want to start eliminating what you own. Colwin points out what I had already discovered, that a cheese slicer serves well as a spatula; a wine bottle can be used as a rolling pin, the sum of a double boiler is less than its parts, which you will use much more frequently; and here's one I hadn't thought of—a coffee grinder can be used to grind nuts and spices. I don't own a coffee grinder. I guess that's why I needed a mini-processor.

I have a dear friend in Montreal who haunts garage sales; his preferred hunting ground is in Westmount and he can get you anything. I'm sure if you needed tin cornucopias, he could find them for you. It just might take a while. Garage sales and flea markets are a form of social satire in today's economy, offering tangible, silly examples of North American civilization. I mean, who really needs a mushroom brush?

CHAPTER THREE

Nutrition

Only Irish coffee provides in a single glass all four essential food groups: alcohol, caffeine, sugar, and fat.

~ Alex Levine

*T*here used to be an incantation like the "something borrowed, something blue" clothing ritual prescribed for a bride that had to do with the perfect menu. If your meal contained all of the following then it was considered aesthetically as well as nutritionally correct:

° something textured

° something creamy

° something crisp

° something sharp

° something sweet

Of course, you could fulfil all these requirements with a peanut butter sandwich on whole wheat bread, a glass of milk, an apple and a piece of cinnamon-flavoured gum. That's missing the point if you're a gourmet cook but it's very reassuring if you're single, don't like spending much time in the kitchen and are addicted to food.

There's a thicket of advice out there about nutrition and you have to pick your way through it. It can get very confusing because food experts change their minds frequently, or contradict each other. Seldom do they eat their words. Nor should you. You can't remember everything they tell you, so go for the most important:

° cut down on salt (and sugar)

° go easy on the fat

° get enough calcium, vitamins
  and fibre

Stick *Canada's Food Guide to Healthy Eating* (free from your local Health Canada office) on your fridge door and eat according to its recommendations: 5 to 12 servings of grain products per day; 5 to 10 servings of fruit and vegetables per day; milk products according to your age, gender and activity; 2 to 3 daily servings of meat and alternatives—and we'll get to those. Trust me, by the time you've eaten all that fibre, you won't have much room to stuff yourself with no-nos.

One thing we're all addicted to, single or not, is salt. We're being told now to take it right off the dinner table.[1] The first hint I had that salt is not all that good for you was when my father had a heart attack. He was prescribed a salt substitute, low in sodium. Then, during one pregnancy, when I was in danger of edema, I was denied salt for a time. Now, of course, thanks to the continuous discoveries and the constant threats that nutritionists make, we all know that we should go easy on the salt. Campbell's soup

1 *IT WASN'T ALWAYS SO
UNWELCOME. SO VALUABLE WAS
IT THAT ROMAN SOLDIERS USED
TO BE PAID IN PRECIOUS SALT—
THE ORIGIN OF THE WORD
SALARY. IT WAS SO HIGHLY
PRIZED IT USED TO BE KEPT
UNDER LOCK AND KEY.*

2 WHY IS IT THAT WHEN THEY TAKE THINGS OUT OF THINGS IT COSTS MORE?

3 SEVERAL YEARS AGO A FRIEND GAVE ME A COOKBOOK OF RECIPES ADAPTED FROM THE FIFTEENTH CENTURY, ACCOMPANIED BY A BOX OF THE RELEVANT HERBS AND SPICES LIKE CUBEBS AND HYSSOP AND SAFFRON, DRIED ELDERBERRIES AND SO ON. I COOKED THE MEAL, INCLUDING TRENCHERS FOR EACH PERSON— DINNER PLATES MADE OF BREAD TO SERVE THE FOOD ON. (THAT'S HOW I LEARNED WHERE THE PHRASE "A GOOD TRENCHER-MAN" COMES FROM.)
WE HAD LITTLE PORK SAUSAGE HORS D'OEUVRES FRIED WITH APPLES AND CINNAMON; THE MAIN COURSE WAS CHICKEN

comes in expensive low-sodium varieties now, as do a lot of products.[2]

Salt, of course, was a blessing, enabling people to preserve food as they had never been able to do, and also to mask the gamier qualities of over-hung meat or food past its prime, though still, I suppose, safe to eat. Salt and smoke long preceded refrigeration and freezing as preservatives. Smoke now is an extravagance, a treat, when used to smoke salmon or oysters or goldeye, and we eat those delicacies in small quantities, ah, but smoked hams and pork and turkeys are still served in larger than bite-sized proportions. Don't forget *hangikjert*, now considered a delicacy in Iceland. It's smoked lamb, served on festive occasions in memory of the times when meat hanging from the rafters of the cooking room smoked by accident over the fire, thus preserving it and staving off hunger for a while longer. How taste buds change, have changed, will change again. Change is on the tip of your tongue.[3]

Go ahead and experiment. Use less and less salt until you get used to going without. Try out other spices and condiments and give your taste buds a lift. It's not as if you're going to suffer from salt deprivation. There's still more than enough salt in food, both naturally present and artificially implanted in the products we buy. We're hardly going to dry up and blow away.

When you first cut out salt, everything tastes like cardboard, but after you get used to it and try salt again, everything tastes like salt (ditto with sugar). What happens is that food starts to taste like itself. It doesn't take that long for this amazing change in your taste buds to take place: from six weeks to three months and you'll have a changed tongue. I do not cook with salt now, except when I start a stock pot and then I use about half of what I did. I do not salt food at table, with the exception of a poached egg, which I eat about four times a year, and fresh beefsteak tomatoes in the summer when I make my annual toasted lettuce and tomato sandwich: no mayo now, and no bacon, but I still use freshly ground black pepper. I always disapproved of people who automatically reach for the salt and pepper before they even taste the food in front of them—especially when I was the one who had prepared the food and who prided herself on her exquisite taste buds.

Fat is another thing you love to hate these days. Fat is not bad if you don't eat too much of it. You still need it for good health and skin. Fat works as a carrier for the fat-soluble vitamins (A, D, E and K) and supplies two essential acids, linoleic and alpha-linolenic, which can come only from food. I'm not going into any more detail than that, because neither of us will remember it. If you decide you want to keep track, get a fat-counter book like I did and work it out.

In the 1980s, during the great Muffin Mania, everyone thought all that bran (read: fibre) was good for you, neglecting to notice that a load of fat came with it. There's as much fat in a large commercial muffin as there is in a doughnut. In fact, you'd be better off eating a six-ounce steak with veg, baked potato and sour cream for 11 grams of fat as compared to 16 in the muffin. If you're devoted to muffins, make your own in a smaller, lower-fat variety (see p. 110)—they freeze well. Now everyone is on a bagel kick, because there's only 1 gram of fat in a bagel—but watch out for the cream cheese! Even so-called light can be very heavy, with 2.5 grams in a tablespoon.

COOKED IN MILK AND HONEY, SEASONED WITH SAFFRON. NOT A GRAIN OF SALT, NOT A HINT OF GARLIC IN THE ENTIRE MEAL—A CHANGE FROM WHAT WE WERE USED TO. THE TASTE IN THE MOUTH AFTER DINNER WAS HIGH AND ROUND, IF YOU UNDERSTAND ME, INSTEAD OF LOW AND THICK. IT MADE ME REALIZE HOW MIGHTILY OUR TASTES HAVE CHANGED IN THE WESTERN WORLD.

Here's a list of lower-fat substitutes for higher-fat foods, culled from a number of sources, to serve as a guideline for you when you're reaching for the no-nos.

SMART CHOICES

Choose

- baked tortilla chips, pretzels, cut-up pita
- salsa
- dips with yogurt, low-fat sour cream
- whole-grain breads
- bruschetta (easy on the oil)
- crudités
- dried fruits
- bagels
- shrimp
- chicken and turkey (white meat, skin off)
- mustard, chutney, salsa
- low-fat sauces
- sherbet, frozen yogurt
- ice milk
- fresh fruit
- angel food cake
- meringues

Try To Avoid

° potato chips, regular tortilla chips

° guacamole

° croissants and Danishes

° pâté

° nuts, especially cashews

° coconut

° muffins, doughnuts

° wings, tempura, fried stuff

° duck, goose, marbled beef

° gravy, cream sauces

° ice cream, whipped cream

° cakes, cookies, pastries

Calcium is something everyone needs, especially women. Osteoporosis is the scary threat looming in the lives of older women today. This loss of bone density is what gave witches a bad name, bent as they were, with their dowager's hump, hurpling along as fast as their arthritic limbs could carry them. No wonder they needed a broom! Now we know how important calcium is to maintain strong bones. If you're a young woman, don't think you can ignore this. You're eating for two: young you right now and old you in the future. The more large-bone exercise[4] and the more calcium you take in before menopause, the better you'll be after. You should be getting a minimum of 800 mg a day, more like 1500 if you're over 40. You still need a lot of calcium in your twilight years.

4 LIKE WALKING, EXERCISE THAT PUTS STRESS ON YOUR LARGE BONES, LIKE HIPS. WALKING IS ABOUT THE BEST EXERCISE THERE IS, GENERALLY. IT'S NOT AT THE TOP OF THE LIST OF BONE-BUILDERS BUT IT'S EASY, IT HELPS AND IT DOES A LOT OF OTHER GOOD BESIDES. AND IT DOESN'T JANGLE THINGS LIKE JOGGING DOES.

Lots of vegetables are "calcium-rich," as they say, but what's important is the actual absorption. Newspapers and magazines provide lists of them in little boxes that you can clip and put on your fridge door as a reminder. I notice that broccoli is on every list.

If you like sardines, you're really on your way, crunching all those little bones full of calcium. I could try to think of something nice to do with them, that is, if you really think you'll eat them. If you like sardines you'll eat them on toast like most sensible people.[5]

All your good intentions in the grocery store aren't going to do your body any good if you bring home the food you think you ought to be eating and then let it rot. Be honest, now. You know you ought to sprinkle bran on your cereal, but are you going to do it? "People lie when you ask them what they eat when they're alone," says Laurie Colwin, and I believe her.[6]

So the moment of truth begins when you talk fresh and attempt to introduce more green into your life.

VEGETABLES

artichokes
No one can feel lonely when eating an artichoke.

asparagus
I used to think that I could not eat asparagus without Hollandaise sauce, but I got over it. Now I use a couple of twists of fresh lemon.[7]

5 *OR TRY THEM IN PASTA SAUCE— WITH GREEN ONIONS, HOT PEPPER FLAKES, WHITE WINE, CAPERS AND PARSLEY. EVEN PEOPLE WHO HATE SARDINES LOVE THIS. ED.*

6 *FOR YEARS I'VE BEEN READING AND PEOPLE HAVE BEEN TELLING ME THAT IT'S VERY GOOD FOR YOU TO DRINK HOT WATER AND LEMON FIRST THING IN THE MORNING. I KNOW SOME PEOPLE WHO (SAY THEY) REALLY DO IT, AND GOOD FOR THEM. I THINK ABOUT IT ONCE IN A WHILE, BUT I SHUDDER AND KEEP ON DRINKING TEA. I JUST READ THAT ADDING BLACKSTRAP MOLASSES TO THE MORNING LEMON DOES WONDERS. I DON'T WANT TO KNOW ANY MORE.*

7 *I ALSO USED TO LOVE WHITE ASPARAGUS. I WAS IN GERMANY ONE SPRING WHEN THE WHITE ASPARAGUS WAS IN SEASON AND RESTAURANTS EVERYWHERE FLASHED A SPECIAL NEON SIGN:*

avocado

Experts keep trying to warn you off avocado because it is very high in fat: 27 to 30 grams compared to the trace found in most fruit. But it has a fair amount of vitamins (A and B1) plus calcium, iron and potassium, and it tastes good.

beans, fresh, green and yellow

You can buy a handful just for you, and no leftovers, but don't forget my antipasto (p. 63), just in case.

bean sprouts

Beware the wrapped package. They get old and funny fast. Always rinse well before using, fresh or canned. Chill fresh sprouts in ice water for half an hour if you want them raw in a salad; boil them for 3 minutes if you're going to dump them into egg foo yong or something like that.

beets

Slice leftover cooked beets and put them in a jar with vinegar to cover (apple cider vinegar would be nice). Good with fish.

Beets are good for you, and so are beet greens. When you buy fresh beets be sure to check that the tops are crisp and not wilted. Store the severed beets for another day but eat the beet greens right away. Wash them well and cook in their own moisture for fewer than 5 minutes, turning over at least once. Drain them in a colander and serve with a twist of lemon.

SPARGEL SPARGEL SPARGEL. IT IS ONE OF THE MOST DELICIOUS USELESS VEGETABLES IN THE WORLD. THE VERY ACTION THAT MAKES IT WHITE—MOUNDING UP THE EARTH SO THE STALK NEVER SEES THE SUN—IS THE VERY THING THAT ROBS IT OF ITS NUTRIENTS. NOT A SPARK OF CHLOROPHYLL IN A CARLOAD OF SPARGEL. PITY.

Belgian endive
Excellent finger food, one stem at a time loaded with something good, like salsa or guacamole.

broccoli[8]
Singles find even one large stalk hard to use up. Steam the whole bunch (peeled, cut up) tender-crisp for use one night with an entrée. Save the rest in a gratin dish. Sprinkled with grated mozzarella or Feta-Garlic Crumbles (p. 96) and lightly zapped, it serves another day as lunch or a light supper. Or if there's still too much, use it in a primavera stir-fry (p. 187) dumped over cooked pasta.

Brussels sprouts
I don't like Brussels sprouts, but here's something for my friend who thinks they're comfort food.

8 THERE'S A COOKBOOK CALLED *THE ENCHANTED BROCCOLI FOREST*, BUT THE BROCCOLI RECIPE IS PURE FICTION. YOU'RE SUPPOSED TO STICK LITTLE BROCCOLI FLORETS UPRIGHT IN SOME OTHER FOOD SO IT LOOKS LIKE LITTLE TREES. OH MY.

COMFORTING BRUSSELS SPROUTS

Brussels sprouts

1 frozen chicken soup cube

1 tbsp (15 mL) liquid honey

1 tsp (5 mL) Dijon mustard

2 tbsp (25 mL) chopped peanuts

Wash and trim the sprouts and put them in a microwave dish with the soup cube. Zap them for 2 or 3 minutes until tender-crisp, stirring once. Toss them in the honey-mustard mixture and peanuts and zap again, 1 minute or to taste.

cabbage

Now here's a vegetable you can grow old with while you use it up.[9] Do something! Coleslaw comes to everyone's mind but it, too, tends to be never ending. Change the seasoning and surprise the cabbage with it. Caraway seeds are good, grated carrots, of course, maybe an apple.[10] I developed a fascinating pasta recipe (p. 192). Drop the last of it (still lots) in beef stock with other leftover vegetables, including beets, and call it borscht. Oh dear, now you either have to have a party or get sick.

carrots, of course

In stock, for seasoning; in soup, for eating. Add thin coin-slices to potato and green salads. Steamed, lightly, as a respectable accompaniment to an entrée; raw, as a crudité; grilled or roasted as part of a team with other vegetables, and here's a favourite: grate carrots and toss them in orange juice with a handful of raisins. I can eat this for lunch or for dessert. You can throw in a little pineapple one time, a few pecans another, or sunflower seeds.

cauliflower

Another vegetable that feels like eternity to a single. You have to make a strong moral decision in the store when it is time to buy another cauliflower, and then work at it. Use a few florets with a dip; steam some or a lot of it for

9 DID YOU KNOW THAT ONE MEDIUM CABBAGE WILL YIELD ABOUT 4 CUPS OF COARSELY GRATED RAW MATERIAL?

10 I HAD SOME RASPBERRY VINAIGRETTE IN MY FRIDGE THAT HAD BEEN THERE TOO LONG SO I MIXED IT WITH YOGURT AND TRIED IT ON THE SLAW AND IT WAS GOOD, SO NOW I DO IT ON PURPOSE. IF YOU DON'T HAVE **RASPBERRY VINAIGRETTE**, EVEN JAM WILL DO, BLENDED WITH APPLE CIDER VINEGAR, YOGURT AND/OR LIGHT MAYO.

dinner, and if you did a lot, then purée the leftovers with chicken stock and maybe some curry and use as a soup, hot or cold, depending on the season. Most recently I have begun to dote on:

CAULIFLOWER CURRY

a small amount of cauliflower

frozen chicken soup cubes

1 small onion, chopped

curry powder

1 cooked potato, cut in chunks

1 tbsp (15 mL) sesame seeds

You can start the cauliflower, cut in slightly larger than bite-sized pieces, in a pan with the cubes and soupée them over medium heat, or you can use leftover cauliflower, steamed tender-crisp. When it suits you, push the cauliflower to the side and stir the onion and curry into the soup, adding another cube as necessary. (Of course you can use canned chicken soup if you have to.) Add the potato, introduce the cauliflower again, sprinkle the whole with sesame seeds, cover and cook briefly until everything is hot and friendly.

celery, yes
Ubiquitous and crunchy, if celery isn't good for me, don't tell me.

coriander
One of my new addictions, first encountered in all its strength and glory a few

years ago when I went to Peru and the
Galapagos Islands. See pesto (p. 186).[11]

corn

On the cob, of course, and how wonderful are all the things even a single
can do with leftover cooked corn on
the cob. Never think, because there's
just one of you, that you shouldn't
cook all the corn you bought (you
couldn't have bought *that* much).
Better to cut the uneaten corn off the
cob and do something with it. Toss it
with lima beans for succotash, with
cooked rice to stuff a pepper, with a
little leftover chicken, green onion,
celery for a swift salad. Stir it into
pancake batter for corn fritters, or into
cornmeal mush for double corn
polenta. Mix it with cooked rice, green
onions, grated Cheddar cheese, a little
milk, chili to taste (optional) and bake
for a quick casserole. This will freeze
and live again another day.

cucumber

Samuel Johnson said, "A cucumber
should be well sliced, and dressed with
pepper and vinegar, and then thrown
out, as good for nothing." Much he
knew. Granted, there's little nutritional
value in a cucumber, but it's a great
mixer. It's wonderful, for example, cut
in chunks, in Greek salad. It's perfec-
tion, sliced thin as a dream and layered
into fine white buttered bread, crusts
removed, seasoned with salt and

11 *SOMEONE TOLD ME IF YOU EAT
CORIANDER EVERY DAY OF THE
WEEK TERRIBLE THINGS WILL
HAPPEN TO YOU. I THINK THAT'S
TRUE OF ALMOST ANYTHING,
EXCEPT GARLIC.*

pepper, and served with fond memories of *The Importance of Being Earnest*. This breaks all my rules about butter and salt and white bread, but there are times when one must throw caution to the winds.

eggplant

No one has any illusions about eggplant, nor should one. It has very few vitamins but, eaten regularly, it helps lower cholesterol.[12] The worst thing about eggplant is the way it soaks up oil. There's no stopping it, so don't give it a chance to start. Try it with roasted red peppers (p. 68). The vitamins in the peppers make up for the paucity of the eggplant.

fennel

I've been on a fennel kick lately and love it, both raw and cooked. Use the fronds for garnish the way you waft dill. Cut off the outer stalks and base and slice the bulb with the grain for tossing in salads. Save the fronds and all, for flavour, when you make Roasted Sweet Potato and Veg (p. 207).

garlic

Garlic is mystic, wonderful. Scarcely any nutritional value, but who cares? It's supposed to ward off vampires and colds. Buy a small amount at a time and look for firm, plump buds. Don't buy them if they're sprouting, if you can help it. Some stores don't sell it

12 YOU CAN MAKE A POOR MAN'S CAVIAR WITH EGGPLANT, USING TOMATOES, PARSLEY, OIL, ONIONS, LEMON JUICE, GARLIC AND SO ON, BUT I'D LEAVE IT TO THE POOR MAN IF I WERE YOU. I'D RATHER HAVE ROE ANY DAY, EVEN LUMPFISH.

fast enough. If you do encounter some green shoots, cut them out.

leek

The emblem of Wales, proud insignia that true Welshmen are supposed to wear on St. David's Day to honour the victory of King Cadwallader over the Saxons in 645, leeks achieved gourmet status when some French chef invented leek vinaigrette. Be sure to wash out all the mud from between the layers. Cook them in a little water as briefly as possible so they won't go mushy on you. I try to go easy on the olive oil and salt and savour the black pepper. They taste good, but you're not missing much in the way of nutrients if you'd rather give them a pass.

lettuce, romaine, mesclun, etc.

Everyone's on a designer greens kick these days, with arugula from France, mesclun from California, endive, escarole and so many hybrids of lettuce you wonder if Luther Burbank is still alive.[13] Men who don't like vegetables think they have come around when they start eating salad, but all these greens, while pretty and piquant, have very little food value.[14]

mushrooms

A fungus with flair! Throw away the plastic bag or wrap you brought them home in and put them in a brown

13 THIS JOKE IS FOR PEOPLE OVER 50, OR DEDICATED GARDENERS.

14 I HAVE ONE FRIEND WHOSE FATHER HAS ALWAYS HATED RABBIT FOOD, AS MEN HIS AGE CALL IT, BUT WHO STARTED EATING IT IN SALAD BARS. HE THINKS HE'S EATING SALAD BUT IT'S HIDDEN UNDER THE OTHER STUFF HE PILES ON: BACON BITS, CROUTONS, PARMESAN AND FETA CHEESE, PASTA, OLIVES, SUNFLOWER SEEDS—EVERYTHING BUT THE GREENS. AT THAT, HE MAY BE AHEAD OF THE GAME. SULPHITES, ANYONE?

paper bag (one of your wine bags will do nicely), but don't seal it. They need cool air. Stuffed mushroom caps are delicious, low-calorie and swiftly cooked in the microwave.

STUFFED MUSHROOM CAPS

large mushrooms, as many as suit you

couple of green onions

chopped fresh dill

1 frozen chicken soup cube

Remove the stems from the caps and chop them finely. Snip the green onions over the chopped mushrooms and mix in a little dill to taste. Put the mushroom mixture on a microwave plate, add a chicken soup cube and zap it on Medium-High briefly. Put the caps on a clean plate and spoon the mushroom mixture into the hollows. Pour any liquid from the first plate into and over the mushrooms. Zap again for 1 minute. Delicious.

A few leftover mushrooms (soupéed first) can be added to an omelet, flung into a frittata, chucked into chow mein, hurled at a ratatouille or eased into a vinaigrette. In the latter case, call it

MUSHROOM SALAD

¼ cup (50 mL) olive oil

1 or 2 tbsp (15 or 25 mL) lemon juice

salt and black pepper to taste

¼ tsp (1 mL) dry mustard

1 tsp (5 mL) dried dill

fresh mushrooms, sliced

Stir the dressing with a fork and pour over the mushrooms. Toss gently, cover, and allow to marinate an hour at least.

onion
The great master of ceremonies, the great leveller.[15]

Red onions are delicious in salads. Also, I cut them into almost every roasted vegetable combination I can think of.

parsley
Parsley, said Ogden Nash, "is gharsley." I don't agree. It pops up all over the place. See pesto (p. 185).

parsnip
In My Other Life I used to peel, slice and fry parsnips sprinkled with lots of brown sugar. I shudder now at the thought. I do like parsnips roasted with fennel (see p. 207).

peas
The reason peas are such a cliché is that they were among the first vegetables successfully to be canned. They don't spoil, they travel well, they suit everyone's diet and so on. If the canners could have arranged to have peas grow square instead of round, so they wouldn't roll off the knife, peas would be perfect. At least once a summer it's fun to buy a bag of unshelled peas and

15 I HAD AN AUNT WHO GAVE ME SOME ADVICE BEFORE I GOT MARRIED. SHE TOLD ME IF I WAS OUT ALL DAY FOOLING AROUND (I CAN'T THINK WHAT SHE HAD IN MIND), I SHOULD RACE IN BEFORE MY HUSBAND GOT HOME AND FRY UP A MESS OF ONIONS. THAT WAY, WHEN HE CAME IN MINUTES LATER, HE'D SNIFF APPRECIATIVELY AND THINK I'D BEEN COOKING ALL DAY JUST FOR HIM. SINGLES, THANK HEAVEN, DON'T HAVE TO RESORT TO SUBTERFUGES LIKE THAT.

shell them, eating half of them raw as you work. Cook them in a nest of lettuce leaves in a saucepan with a very little water and 1 tsp (5 mL) sugar. Another cliché is mint with them, and I leave that to your discretion.

I like snow peas that snap in my mouth. They're wonderful in stir-fries. Buy just enough to use up immediately. You don't want to lose that snap.

peppers

A sweet pepper has more vitamin C than an orange. Stuffed peppers make a complete dinner for a single, and use up leftovers besides.

STUFFED PEPPER

1 whole sweet pepper[16], top cut off, seeds removed

frozen chicken soup cube

Filling: choice of

° cooked or canned corn

° cooked rice

° some more green pepper

° green onions

° grated Cheddar or other cheese

° some cooked ground beef

° chopped cooked eggplant

° a little chili?

16 *NOT YELLOW OR ORANGE—THEY TURN A NASTY COLOUR.*

Some people precook their pepper before stuffing it, but I like it crispy. Simply mix a bunch of appropriate food, as suits you and your fridge, and stuff the pepper with it. Put the pepper in a microwave dish, pour a little lubrication in the dish—dare I say chicken soup?—and zap on Medium-High for 3 or 4 minutes. Give it an aftercook of 1 minute. Very filling.

potato
One of the nicest things that happened to diets in recent years is that the potato is allowed back on the table. No oil, no fat, no butter, no sour cream, but beautiful potato, yes!

There's a lot of ways to "fry" a potato without deep fat. Try this one:

OVEN-FRIED POTATOES

1 good-sized baking potato

1 tbsp (15 mL) or less salad (not olive) oil

Seasoning to taste

Peel and slice the potato into french-fry strips and toss in a bowl with the oil and seasonings. Spread out on a nonstick pan and bake for 20 minutes at 350°F (180°C).[17] Turn them and spread them out again and bake another 20 minutes. Test for crispness.

17 *I USE THE BIG OVEN FOR THIS.*

Enjoy these too:

MICRO-BAKED POTATOES

2 smallish new potatoes

3 or 4 cloves garlic, minced

seasoning to taste

1 frozen chicken soup cube OR maybe
1 tsp (5 mL) oil

Peel and slice the potatoes fairly thick and toss with the garlic seasonings, and soup or oil. Zap for 2 minutes on High, stir, zap again till they're cooked, maybe another minute? Potatoes vary, as well as ovens.

Everyone has a favourite potato salad, so I won't bother here. (But see p. 96 if you're in the neighbourhood.)

radish

I used to scoff at radishes until I met a young woman who had worked as an *au pair* for a French family just a few years ago. Times had been hard and it showed in their food. She says she will never forget the night they had hot buttered radishes for dinner. Before that I was feeling romantic about radishes, the big fat kind you see in French cookbooks and movies, eaten with butter and bread and a glass of wine. I made up a sauce for radishes last summer and invited some neighbours to dine with me (we did have more than radishes to eat!)

MARINATED RADISHES

a bunch of big fat radishes

½ cup (125 mL) low-fat yogurt

1 tbsp (15 mL) soy sauce

Cut the radishes into thick slices. Mix the yogurt and soy sauce and toss the radishes in it. Let sit at room temperature for about an hour. It's wet, so serve with a fork, and good bread.

spinach

One bag of spinach suits a single very well. Wash thoroughly, trim off the stems and cook all of it in a covered saucepan, just in its own moisture, for no more than 5 minutes. Drain it and divide it between tonight's dinner plate and a microwave dish that you put into either the freezer or the fridge, well covered. When ready to serve it the second time, zap it for 3 or 4 minutes on Low if it's frozen, 1 or 2 if it's not; then sprinkle it with grated low-fat mozzarella cheese or my Feta-Garlic Crumbles (see p. 96) and hit it again on High until the cheese is all oozy. A bed of this spinach makes a nice base for fish (see p. 166). Spinach also makes a healthy dip blended with yogurt, chopped green onions and 1 garlic clove. Serve it with raw veg.

squash

You can freeze uncooked squash. When you cut and bake and eat the first half, even of a small acorn squash, you may not want to see the other half for some time. Scoop out the seeds, cover the surface with plastic wrap, seal it in a plastic bag and freeze until further notice. I used to bake squash with butter and brown sugar but no more. Pour a little apple syrup into the cavity and

52

season with freshly ground black pepper. Be sure to pierce the sides with a knife before you microwave it—6 to 10 minutes, turning once. The thawed squash doesn't have quite the same texture as when it was fresh, but it's totally edible.

sweet potato, also called yam
They are not interchangeable, but I won't go into the distinction. Sweet potatoes are making a comeback.[18] Forget the abomination Americans have made popular with Thanksgiving dinner, an obscene dish loaded with butter, brown sugar and marshmallows. Sweet potatoes are simply wonderful pierced and baked in the microwave oven for about the same length of time as a white potato (12 minutes in mine), turning once. They mix and mash well, too.

18 "EAT YOUR SWEET POTATOES SO YOU CAN STAY YOUNG LONGER," SAYS MAGGIE WALDRON.

For a mealier potato, sweet or white, pick it up in a tea towel (so as not to burn your fingers) and roll it in your hands before you cut it open.

tomato
I don't need to tell you what to do with a tomato. On the other hand—
To peel a tomato easily, drop it into boiling water for a minute, then into ice water before you pull off the skin.

Every gardener knows about green tomatoes, but singles without a garden are hard pressed to find them. Roadside stands sometimes sell them. If you find some, here's a variation on the usual fried green:

CURRIED "FRIED" GREEN TOMATOES

1 tsp (5 mL) curry powder

1 or 2 frozen chicken soup cubes

3 green tomatoes, sliced fairly thick

In a skillet on medium heat soupée the curry powder in the soup cubes as they thaw and stir it around. Gently cook the tomato slices in the mixture, one layer at a time, turning as necessary, until tender.

turnip
Another large vegetable for the ages. Save it for stew for a crowd. I can only recommend peeling and slicing them incredibly thin to use as a chip for dips. Even then, a little goes a long long way if you can't find a small one. Maybe you could share one with a friend.

zucchini
Soup—especially curried, cold or hot; frittata; ratatouille; or simply sliced thinly and tossed with slivers of green pepper as a delicious salad for one.

FRUIT

A number of people aren't sure how to choose good fruit. When in doubt, ask the produce manager, if you can find him—over there behind the rutabagas. I'll tell you what I know. First of all, I know, and so do you, that the secret to buying good fruit is to buy it in season. Never mind how tempting strawberries in January look, resist! You'll be doing your pocketbook and your taste buds a favour.

apples

There are so many varieties of apple that it's a shame if you and your supermarket are limited to Macs and Delicious. Try others, if you can find them; Spartan, Granny Smith, Golden Delicious are other good eating apples, and for cooking, try to find Jonathan or Gravenstein. The peak season is October through March and as you know, apples keep well. You must buy your apples by the one or two, choosing them for colour and firmness. Don't be deceived by the high gloss of wax. Store in the refrigerator in a plastic bag, but let one come to room temp to enjoy full eating flavour.

If one or two apples go soft on you, peel, quarter and core them and zap them on High for 3 or 4 minutes in the microwave in a shallow bath of maple syrup for a quick, delicious dessert.

apricots

Like jewels, these are, orange-gold in colour, and must be treasured. Choose a handful of plump ones and eat them immediately because they don't keep well.

banana

Full of potassium, low in fat, tastes like dessert. Alternate thin slices of banana and tomato, sprinkled with a little lemon juice, as a side highlight with a curry dish.

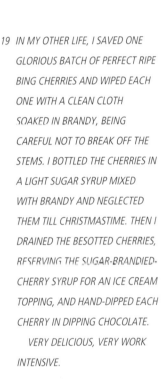

berries
Strawberries are supposed to be the most popular fruit of all. Great alone, or with chocolate, or champagne. Try a dip of yogurt laced with Grand Marnier. Simplest of all is to dip them first in low-fat sour cream and then in brown sugar.

cherries
Wonderful to eat out of hand.[19]

clementines
Easy to eat, delicious with chocolate fondue.

grapes
Did you know there are 10 calories in a grape?

grapefruit
A thin skin means more juice. Try it hot for dessert: top a half with ½ tsp (2 mL) liquid honey, sprinkle with cinnamon and zap for a minute.

kiwi
Ripe when yielding to thumb pressure. If underripe when you bring them home, store them at room temperature in a plastic bag in company with an apple. Good with low-fat cottage cheese for lunch, colourful and good with strawberries, or sliced on the side with a curry.

kumquats
Dried-up and merely decorative in northern markets, the best kumquats are

19 IN MY OTHER LIFE, I SAVED ONE GLORIOUS BATCH OF PERFECT RIPE BING CHERRIES AND WIPED EACH ONE WITH A CLEAN CLOTH SOAKED IN BRANDY, BEING CAREFUL NOT TO BREAK OFF THE STEMS. I BOTTLED THE CHERRIES IN A LIGHT SUGAR SYRUP MIXED WITH BRANDY AND NEGLECTED THEM TILL CHRISTMASTIME. THEN I DRAINED THE BESOTTED CHERRIES, RESERVING THE SUGAR-BRANDIED-CHERRY SYRUP FOR AN ICE CREAM TOPPING, AND HAND-DIPPED EACH CHERRY IN DIPPING CHOCOLATE.
VERY DELICIOUS, VERY WORK INTENSIVE.

20 IN MY OTHER LIFE I ACTUALLY
SPLIT A FEW DOZEN KUMQUATS
AND STUFFED THEM WITH CREAM
CHEESE. I FORGET WHY.

picked fresh off their own small tree.[20]
Ambience is all, even more than
ripeness.

mangoes

I suppose we aren't meant to be
addicted to tropical fruit, but there it
is. In the summer (in a northern clime)
mix a couple of peeled sliced mangoes
with fresh blueberries, cultivated or
wild. Beautiful colour, beautiful taste.
The more colour in the skin, the riper
the fruit.

melons

If you can smell that delicious aroma,
the fruit is ripe. Sliced cantaloupe with
low-fat cottage cheese is a delicious
summer lunch. Squeeze a wedge of lime
over a Persian or honeydew melon.
No sugar.

nectarines

A peach without a five-o'clock shadow.
Buy your nectarines when ripe or nearly
so. Green fruit will only shrivel. Don't
peel, but wash well.[21]

21 DID YOU KNOW YOU CAN BUY
SPECIAL SOAP FOR FRUIT AND
VEGETABLES NOW TO CLEAN OFF
THE CHEMICALS? AI, SUCH A
WORLD!

oranges

Fruit that feels heavy, with thin skins,
is the juiciest. The number on oranges
refers to the size: the number that will
fit in a crate. Small oranges are often a
good buy. Don't store too long in the
fridge as they will dry out. Better in a
cool place, 40° to 60°F (5° to 15°C).

papaya

When fully ripe, it's soft enough to dent slightly on thumb pressure. Chill, cut in quarters and serve with lime wedges.

peaches

Some people[22] gag on peach fuzz and must be catered to. Cover a bunch of peaches with boiling water and then ice water and they'll peel easily. Cut them up and toss with a little lemon juice to prevent them from darkening. You still can't beat peaches and cream and sugar, decadent though it is.

Even more decadent and also addictive is **Peach Melba**, named after the Australian opera singer. Buy the best vanilla ice cream you can find and arrange a couple of poached peach halves on top (lightly cooked in a sugar syrup: 2 cups/500 mL water to 2 tbsp/25 mL sugar, but I hate to tell you, canned peaches, drained, taste much the same). Pour raspberry purée over all. (Make a quick **raspberry purée** by pushing thawed frozen raspberries through a sieve fine enough to catch the seeds. It's worth it.)

22 *MY CHILDREN.*

pears

With no fruit must one be more careful than with pears. You almost have to make an appointment to eat them. Never never buy too many. Buy ripe—

yielding to the thumb—and take *it* home and eat it. See p. 227 for a lovely pear recipe for guests.

pineapple
Ripe is more brown-gold than green. If you hold one up by a centre leaf and it pulls itself loose (field it with your other hand), it should be ready to eat. Smell it, too. I like it with low-fat cottage cheese; chunks are good tossed in that carrot-raisin salad (see p. 41).

plums
Eat out of hand, but wash well.

watermelon
I don't like watermelon.

There, that's the fruit and vegetable lineup. Most people like fruit more than vegetables and you probably do, too. It's nature's comfort food. You have to face a few incontrovertible facts about yourself. Good nutrition or not, you eat what you like. Hey, it's your mouth and more to the point here, it's your life. You're grown up now. You've lived with oughts and shoulds all your life. Surely now that you're on your own in the kitchen you have a right to make your own realistic decisions about your lifestyle, which includes, of course, your eating and cooking habits. Just so you don't get scurvy.

CHAPTER FOUR

Stocking Up

*Be prepared to use anything that comes
to hand, but also be sure to have on
hand what you want to be prepared with.*

~ *Betty Jane Wylie*

B*efore* you stock up on non-perishables, you have
to empty out. Extend your spring or fall cleaning to
your kitchen, especially your fridge, but do it alone.[1]
The inside of a refrigerator is terribly, embarrass-
ingly intimate. You can learn a lot about people
from their fridges. I could tell you horror stories that
would make your saliva run cold, of dried-up car-
casses, cheese like hard bars of soap, tangled green
onions, limp abandoned celery, grainy Christmas
hard sauce (in July), fermenting orange juice, little
dishes filled with blue fur or—worse—unnameable
things that *move*! But I won't. Just let me say that
your refrigerator is an integral part of happy, thrifty
cooking and you have to let it know who's in charge.

Singles' fridges are literal manifestations of several of Life's Rules, only slightly paraphrased to suit

1 *THIS IS ANOTHER ONE OF THE
TIMES YOU ARE REALLY GLAD
YOU LIVE ALONE.*

the circumstances. Paul Dickson has collected the official rules and the official explanations in two useful books that have nothing to do with cooking but that explain many of life's dilemmas encountered in the kitchen. I have extrapolated from them and come up with some logical extensions of my own.

For example, here's a rule that applies to every single's fridge I have ever known: *Bottles multiply to fill the door shelves available.* One of the main reasons for this is that the owner has only one mouth and can't consume fast enough to keep up.[2] Even a small size of something lasts forever in a single's fridge. Let me list the contents of a fridge door—mine, probably similar to yours. This may get a little too explicit for some people. If you don't have a strong stomach, skip this part. The pong of some people's fridges has to be smelled to be believed.

2 OR BEFORE BOREDOM SETS IN AND SOMETHING ELSE STRIKES THE FANCY TASTE BUD.

THE DOOR SHELF STORY

3 ONE OF THE NICEST THINGS ABOUT MY CHILDREN GROWING UP IS THAT I WILL NEVER HAVE TO EAT ANOTHER HOT DOG.

Dijon mustard

honey mustard

hot dog mustard???[3]

On your way to using things up: a teaspoon of a piquant mustard livens up a low-fat cheese omelet.

garlic mustard, probably a gift, as is that cute trio of

gourmet mustards on the bottom shelf (they're not your fault)

chutney, Major Grey (my favourite)

home-made pear chutney, another gift

jalapeño peppers, sliced, two jars (I forgot I had one and bought another)

low-fat "free" salad dressings, two
bottles

fancy salad dressing, the last of a set of
three   another gift [4]

Szechuan sauce, without which I cannot
live

framboise preserves in champagne
(gift)

lingonberries in sugar (yet another gift)

real maple syrup, which goes quickly

unsweetened apple syrup, which
doesn't

light imitation maple syrup—what can
I say?

white wine, an opened bottle, vacuum-
stoppered

Perrier water, open

fruit vinaigrette, another gift, wonderful
spicy stuff, which, replenished several
times with apple cider vinegar, has lost
its kick and has to go. I'll miss it.

capers

beet horseradish

hoisin sauce

fermented black bean sauce with garlic

mint jelly and mint sauce, both from
the days when I ate more lamb than I
do now

4 I THINK HOME-MADE RELISHES,
JAMS AND JELLIES AND
GOURMET-SHOP SAUCES, MUS-
TARDS AND DRESSINGS—ALL
GIFTS—ARE AS UBIQUITOUS IN
FRIDGE SHELVES AS
OLD SPICE AFTERSHAVE, PACO
RABANE COLOGNE, BATH OIL PEL-
LETS AND BODY LOTIONS—ALL
GIFTS—ARE IN THE BATHROOM.

Thank goodness I no longer own a fridge with an egg rack in the door allowing space for *nine* eggs. The designers finally realized that not only was it an irrelevant number for eggs but the eggs would be happier and safer if allowed to rest covered in their box until used.

There are little cabinets in my fridge door for butter and shortening, which I no longer use, and cheese, which I keep elsewhere,[5] so these store pine nuts and reserve packages of unopened coffee. No chocolate, though—sauce or frosting or bars—and no Oreos in the freezer, either, I'm happy to report. I know several chocoholics whose fridges must be hyperglycemic. Mine is okay, and fairly fat-free. Would I could say the same of myself.

In *The Seven Year Itch*, the movie character played by Marilyn Monroe kept her girdle in the fridge so it would be cool when she put it on. In *The faux Gourmet*, Juli Huss describes the contents of a character's refrigerator:

> 4 bottles of Chanel nail polish
>
> 3 pairs of Christian Dior pantyhose
>
> 1 package of Eveready batteries
>
> 1 can of Slimfast
>
> ½ can of Diet Coke
>
> an empty package of peanut M&Ms

I interviewed an older single woman who was quite dismayed with the contents of her fridge.[6] It looked pretty full, she said, but then she realized that there was nothing to eat. You don't often hear a woman say that. Men can look in a full fridge and say there's nothing to eat, but most women know better. Still, she had another point to make: a fridge for one

5 IN A PLASTIC BOX THAT WAS ONCE A CONTAINER FOR ICE IN A FORMER FRIDGE THAT ENJOYED MAKING ITS OWN ICE CUBES; THE MORAL IS, DON'T THROW AWAY ANY STORAGE ITEM.

6 THIS WOMAN, BY THE WAY, KEPT OLIVE OIL IN HER FRIDGE, NOT A GOOD IDEA. IT THICKENS, GETS CLOUDY AND TASTES DIFFERENT. SINGLES SHOULD NEVER BUY LARGE ECONOMY SIZES OF OLIVE OIL, UNLESS THEY WANT TO

seldom looks like it, with all the jars and bottles hanging around. It's empty, but it looks crowded.

Here's another Wylie Conclusion: *A fridge for one is like a part-time job*—unreal. Actually, sometimes it's surreal. Just as work expands over and beyond the time allotted to it, so the entire contents of a refrigerator threaten to take over the available space. It's those bottles that do us all in! The trick is to find ways to empty them with a clear conscience.

Here's a wonderful way to cope. The point of this operation is to empty your fridge door shelves, use up any leftover vegetables you have lying around (if you don't, then use a drained can of cut-up green beans) and clear out your condiment cupboard. Take inventory of your bottles and jars and see what you can muster to put into this never-to-be-repeated antipasto. What about cocktail onions? Another jar gone.

BATHE IN IT, BECAUSE SHELF LIFE IS NOT GREAT. IF YOU CAN'T RESIST A BARGAIN, YOU COULD ALWAYS INCREASE YOUR CONSUMPTION BECAUSE OLIVE OIL IS PRETTY GOOD FOR YOU. IT'S A MONOUNSATURATED FAT, HEART-HEALTHIER THAN BUTTER ON YOUR FRENCH OR ITALIAN BREAD, AND DELICIOUS WHEN SEASONED WITH GARLIC OR ROSEMARY. BETTER (THINNER) THAN SLOOSHING IT ON THE BREAD OR PLATE, THOUGH, TRY PAINTING IT ON WITH A SMALL BRUSH.

FRIDGE DOOR ANTIPASTO

cooked green and/or wax beans

cooked carrots

1 can (10 oz/284 mL) button mushrooms

stuffed olives

pitted ripe olives

sweet mixed pickles

cocktail onions

1 tin (4.7 oz/133 g) water-packed tuna, drained

chili sauce

salsa

ketchup

tomato sauce or paste

juice of a lemon

horseradish

Worcestershire sauce

celery

7 A STOCK POT COLLECTION IS DIVIDED INTO TWO PARTS: WET AND DRY, SORT OF. ANY TIME YOU CHOP OFF THE LEAVES AND ROUGH PARTS OF CELERY, THE TOP AND BOTTOM OF A CARROT OR TURNIP OR PARSNIP, PEEL A POTATO, TRIM A LEEK—WHATEVER—PUT THE DISCARD MATERIAL INTO A PLASTIC BAG IN THE FREEZER. THIS IS RAW MATERIAL FOR YOUR NEXT SOUP STOCK. (SEE BASIC STOCK, P. 103). ANY TIME YOU DRAIN A CAN OF VEGETABLES OR HAVE VEGETABLE WATER LEFT FROM COOKING, SAVE THAT LIQUID IN A CONTAINER IN THE FREEZER. (DITTO FOR FISH, FROM POACHING—SAVE SEPARATELY FOR FISH STOCK.) FREEZE THE VEGETABLE STOCK IN CUBES, JUST

Pile the leftover cooked beans and carrots, cut small, into a large bowl. You should have about 1 to 1½ (250 to 375 mL) cups of veg. Add the mushrooms, drained (freeze the liquid in cubes or add it to your stock pot collection),[7] and up to ½ cup (125 mL) each of stuffed olives, ripe olives, sweet mixed pickles, cutting them up if some of them are too large, and cocktail onions. Now add the tuna, and then dump in whatever you can find to make up 1½ cups (375 mL) and a half cup or so of something with a tomato base and lots of zing: chili sauce, salsa, a sloosh from a ketchup bottle, tomato sauce/paste, lemon juice, horseradish, a dash of Wooster. Chop up the celery—about 1 cup (250 mL)—and toss it in. Now gently stir the mess with a wooden spoon or a rubber spatula so as not to cut anything. Pack it in a couple of large covered jars or crocks in the fridge to allow the occupants' acquaintance to ripen into friendship—a few hours or a day. To serve, mound an individual serving on a lettuce leaf to eat as a fork-food antipasto, or serve it in a small bowl surrounded by crackers to pile it on. If it's too much for you to use up, even with guests, pack it in an attractive jar and give it to someone else.[8]

You'll get more juice from a lemon if you let it sit in hot water for a couple of minutes and roll it in your hands before squeezing.

AS YOU DO YOUR CHICKEN STOCK, AND COOK WITH IT, INSTEAD OF OIL.

8 I DON'T WANT TO HEAR ANY MORE ABOUT IT.

You may not have the same ingredients as listed here; even if you do, you'll never have that exact combination again. You only have to understand the principle of what you're doing: creating an edible mélange of pleasing tastes. One caution: if you don't like something all by itself, don't throw it in the pot, because you still won't like it. Be honest and save yourself some money in the long run by having the courage to throw things out. Just remember what you tossed so you won't make the same mistake twice.

This next one takes more courage to make but you'll be glad you did.

FRIDGE DOOR BARBECUE SAUCE

plum sauce

salsa

horseradish

chili sauce

bottled barbecue sauce

soy sauce (not too much)

jelly (not too much)

you know your fridge better than I do

1 onion, diced

1 can (10 oz/284 mL) tomato soup

Empty the contents of all your old bottles and jars—except the ones with mould, which you can toss—into a blender or large processor bowl. Add onion and the tomato soup, to make you feel you are contributing something. Blend it all and taste it. You may feel it's missing something: if you want sweet, add honey; if sharp, add apple cider vinegar. What you have now is an incredible barbecue sauce, best for spareribs, which are the ultimate in finger foods.

> *If you live in an apartment that bans balcony barbecuing, take heart. You don't have to barbecue to have barbecued spareribs. Marinate and then roast spareribs in this sauce for an hour in a 350°F (180°C) oven. Separate the ribs, arrange them on a pan, paint on some more sauce and broil them just to get them crispy and finger-lickin' good. If you share these with anyone (children? a close friend?) and they should ask you for the recipe, smile inscrutably. You'll never be able to repeat it.*

Now put all those glass jars and bottles in the Blue Box and feel grateful for your recycled shelves.

So much for the refrigerator. On to the cupboards. It's stocking up time.

Singles have to develop a siege mentality. It's not tomorrow they're concerned about, it's tonight's dinner. If you're tired, broke, running late or simply don't feel like cooking, do you have something on hand that will stave off hunger tonight? Most practical cookbooks list basic staples you should have in the cupboards but they neglect to translate the list into fast, edible food. I'm not saying you have to have an exhaustive supply of food, just some odds and ends that appeal to you that you might orchestrate into a meal in a pinch. I'm going to add comments to my list to enable you to start composing.

ON THE SHELF

A sampling of possible canned goods

Vegetables and Beans

artichoke bottoms

One poached egg, trimmed and chilled, on one artichoke bottom, with Hollandaise sauce (canned or packaged) or bottled salsa on top equals one gorgeous hors d'oeuvre for unexpected company. Two per serving, sprinkled with grated Parmesan cheese, swiftly broiled, and you have brunch.

artichoke hearts

Toss with couscous from a mix for a quick dinner, or heat in a mixture of cooked wild rice (from a mix) and a can of cream of celery soup for ditto.

black beans

Combine drained beans with roasted peppers and hot or mild seasoning for a salad (ripen for three hours in the fridge; keeps for five days), or add chopped canned jalapeño peppers and sautéed chopped onions, season to taste and mix with cooked brown rice (mix or leftover) for a vegetarian dinner with complementarity.[9]

9 A BALANCE OF AMINO ACIDS AMOUNTING TO A COMPLETE PROTEIN. NUTRITIONISTS AREN'T AS RABID ABOUT COMPLEMENTARITY AS ADELLE DAVIS USED TO BE.

*You can buy bottled or
deli roasted peppers but they're expensive.*

ROASTED RED PEPPERS

*Wash and cut several red peppers in half lengthwise,
clean out the seeds and lay peppers cut side down in a roasting pan. Roast them for 20 to 30 minutes at 375°F (190°C).
If the skin's not looking damaged enough, give them a little
longer. (Some people broil the peppers until they're charred
but then they're a mess to handle.) Put them into a brown
paper bag (use tongs because they're very hot) and let them
rest for 20 minutes. This makes them easier to peel. Then
skin them and slice into thumb-wide pieces and put them in
a shallow dish. Dribble a little olive oil over them and maybe
some salt (sometimes I do, sometimes I don't). That's all.
They are so comforting!*

chick peas

You need a recipe for hummus:

HUMMUS

1 can (19 oz/540 mL) chick peas, drained

¼ cup (50 mL) tahini

2 tbsp (25 mL) lemon juice or 1 fresh lemon, squeezed

4 cloves garlic, crushed

freshly ground black pepper

pinch of salt (optional)

lots of parsley

Blend the ingredients in a food processor and pile in a bowl for dipping with warmed torn-up pita bread or raw vegetables. Obviously this is too much for one person. I'm working on it.

green beans
Drain and heat with slivered almonds for an emergency vegetable. No almonds? Try sunflower seeds or peanuts.

kidney beans
Most commonly used in chili, but smash them with salsa and spread them over nachos, top with grated cheese and zap them in the microwave for an indulgent pig-out.

lentils
Sauté chopped onion and apple in curry, stir in drained canned lentils and heat for a quick hot meal. For a cold one, prepare bulgur according to package directions, combine with drained lentils and a collection of chopped crunchy stuff: pepper (yellow is pretty), celery, cucumber, green onions, a little red onion, maybe an olive or two. Toss with a dressing consisting of olive oil, lemon juice, crushed garlic, dill, parsley and mint mixed with a minimum of salt and freshly ground black pepper. Serve with some decorative tomato wedges and a crumble of feta cheese on top. Lukewarm is okay; in the fridge, covered, it ripens well.

If you need only a small amount of a large onion, make cuts across but not through at right angles and then slice it for instant dice. Wrap what's left in plastic wrap and store in the fridge. I've never figured out a way not to cry over an onion: not with a burnt matchstick or stale bread in my mouth, or under cold running water, or upside down—the onion, not me—so I just weep a little.

lima beans
Everyone always thinks succotash (lima beans, green onions and corn, lots of black pepper) when they think lima beans, and you can too, but they're also good heated with a little cut-up ham or bacon or chicken in a cream of some-thing soup with some green pepper for colour and crunch.

mushrooms

Stems and pieces—only one can, but it may come in handy to extend or substi-tute for a small amount of leftover meat.

olives
Black, pitted—for Greek salad, one of my addictions. If you buy them canned, as I must, refrigerate in a jar after opening. Pour off half the brine and replace it with olive oil, adding at least 2 tsp (10 mL) dried oregano. Wonderful marinade, which you can use for your Greek salad dressing.

pinto beans
Good in chili, with or without the carne, but try them as a salad when you don't

have greens, tossing canned corn
niblets and a sliced onion in a sweet,
sharp dressing.

*Pour boiling water over thinly sliced onion to sweeten it
(and make it easier to digest). Drain and chill (in the
freezer if you're short of time) before tossing in salad.*

pork and beans
You probably have a favourite way of
spiking canned beans.

Try canned pineapple chunks, peanuts and a sloosh of honey mustard for
a change.

Fish

clams
Canned, minced, perfect for a fast fast
pasta sauce.

salmon
Be sure to eat the bones of canned
salmon—full of calcium. Mash them in
when you're making sandwich filling or
a quickie salmon loaf: 7.5 oz/213 g
canned salmon mashed with ¼ cup
(50 mL) cracker or dry bread crumbs,
bound with 1 egg beaten with ½ cup
(125 mL) milk, and seasoned with
pepper, and 1 tsp (5 mL) dried dill.
Pack in a small buttered loaf pan and
bake 1 hour at 350°F (180°C). Serve
with sauce: maybe a cheese and
broccoli soup?

shrimp
Good as an additive, tucked around fillets of sole baked in cream of mushroom soup thinned with sherry, topped with Parmesan cheese and baked or zapped. Process canned shrimp with yogurt and dill for a quick cold dip, or with cheese soup and garlic for a hot one, zapped for two minutes before serving—with rice crackers, perhaps.

tuna
Water-packed. Everyone knows what to do with tuna fish in a sandwich, but what about making mayonnaise out of it? Process with 4 or 5 anchovy fillets,[10] a little lemon juice, a few grinds of black pepper and as little olive oil as you can get away with, for a mixture you'd even like to spread on tree bark and lick off. This is an imitation of *tonnato*, the sauce that classically graces cold roast veal. Use it for an elegant dip. And yes, it freezes, but you could thin what's left (with lemon juice? buttermilk? clam juice?) and toss it with cooked pasta. Num.

10 *I KNOW, I KNOW, WHAT DO YOU DO WITH THE REST OF THE ANCHOVIES? WRAP THEM TIGHTLY IN FOIL, FREEZE THEM, AND USE THEM WITHIN A MONTH.*

Fruit

mandarin oranges
Good to add to a spinach salad, with or without shrimp

pineapple, crushed
For a quick glaze, mix with hot mustard and spread over a hunk of back bacon

to bake for an hour at 350°F (180°C). Brunch/supper. Also provides the sweet in a sweet-and-sour sauce for shrimp and, if you must, one of the sauces to be spooned over assorted ice creams for a sinful banana split.

Soups

I know, they're salty. These are for emergencies, self-explanatory and they'll come up in the natural course of things:

- ° beef broth

- ° broccoli-cheese

- ° cheese

- ° chicken broth

- ° clam chowder

- ° cream of celery

- ° cream of cliché[11]

- ° minestrone (stir in pesto, p. 184)

- ° tomato (quick base for chili or spaghetti sauce)

11 *THAT'S MUSHROOM TO PEOPLE WHO DIDN'T LIVE THROUGH THE GREAT CASSEROLE RENAISSANCE*

Grains and Rice

bulgur
Available as a mix, easily prepared, makes your wonderful tabbouleh (which has its own seasoned mix) but can also be stirred into chili instead of rice.

couscous

This used to take longer to prepare, with all that boiling water and stand-ing, but now it's 7 minutes from the package to wonderful, nutritious com-binations using your emergency shelves or your imagination. Stir in green onions and canned (rinsed) chick peas, raisins, grated fresh ginger and fresh coriander, or pile in the sautéed garlic and sliced red peppers and top with a little cooked chicken or fish or lamb (we're talking leftovers again).

oatmeal

The 3-minute kind (mix it with oat bran—good for you) cooks in the microwave with maple syrup for an instant delicious breakfast. Add a clutch of raisins for extra nutrition.

popcorn

Apparently popcorn isn't the enemy we think it is. Without butter, it's extremely low-fat and low-calorie and it provides a surprising amount of protein. Still, I wouldn't recommend dinner with Orville more than once a month. Keep the magic.

quinoa

A for Addictive. This ancient grain—pronounced keen-wa—the only one that supplies a complete amino acid, is adaptable to main course, breakfast and dessert, and absolutely delicious. More anon.

rice
° basmati—not as nutritious but
  delicious
° brown—the best, nutty and healthful. Allow more time for cooking.
  Cook 2 cups (500 mL) of it on Sunday
  and use the extra during a week
  you plan on having leftover chicken
  or fish.
° mix with different seasonings, sometimes useful, especially the wild and
  brown rice combination
° white, short-grain, good for rice
  pudding
° wild—expensive but delicious. Don't
  buy the precooked stuff, it's awful.

Nuts and Seeds

peanuts

Shelled—so useful for so many things,
to blend into pestos, sprinkle in chili,
chop into an accompaniment for a curry
or make your own quickie **Szechuan
sauce**: micro-process a handful of
peanuts with a couple of splashes of
soy sauce and apple cider vinegar, and
2 tbsp (25 mL) liquid honey.

pecans
Good in my version of Waldorf salad.

WYLIE WALDORF

Peel, core and cut an apple into bite-sized chunks and toss in a salad bowl with a little lemon juice—to prevent it from premature aging, and it's the only dressing you're going to get. Add bite-sized pieces of celery equal to the amount of the apple, and a handful of whole pecans. Fork in (i.e., scrape with a fork, allowing the pieces to drop into the bowl) a hunk of blue cheese. Toss. That's all.

pine nuts
My best pesto pal. Store an overage of nuts in the freezer so they won't go rancid.

Next, **the Staples**

For a sweeter fridge, buy an extra box of baking soda, open it and store unobtrusively on the bottom shelf at the back.

baking powder

baking soda

Bisquick
Few singles can survive without a biscuit mix in their cupboard. In My Other Life I used to make my own.[12] Even though you have somethin' lovin' from the oven in your freezer, you still need this mix, to assemble your own large shortcakes, chicken pie toppings and Beef Roll-Ups.

12 I WAS INSUFFERABLE.

BEEF ROLL-UPS

Grind up or mince leftover beef (steak, roast) with an onion, seasoning to taste and enough ketchup or salsa to bring it to spreading consistency. Make up your dough according to package directions, roll it out and slather the meat mixture all over it. Roll it into a cylinder, cut it into 2-inch (5 cm) slices (like a cinnamon bun), and lay them in a greased baking pan. Bake about 35 minutes at 350°F (180°C). A very '50s recipe.

cereal
personal choice

chocolate
Semi-sweet is handier to have on hand than unsweetened, and if you have to make a choice, chips rather than the packaged individual blocks, for swift chocolate dips or filling for frozen ready-to-bake croissants or a swift fondue or a blender mousse. (Scratch the mousse; people always think it's Jell-O Pudding.) You don't need me to tell you what to do with chocolate, but I will before I'm through.

crackers
Personal choice, but have you tried rice crackers? Good with that swift dip made with (canned) shrimp (page 72).

flour
Preferably whole wheat. Granted, we don't use much flour in its primal state these days, but it's nice to have in case you need to make flour-and-water paste for some creative children who drop by,

or cookies for same. Or pancakes from scratch.

All purpose: Keep a large shaker-full handy for dusting the counter when you make Bisquick biscuits, and for the roux later, etc.

honey
E for Essential, loved by the ancient Romans and still popular after all these centuries. Not a low-calorie sweetener but a nutritious, useful one.

jams and jellies
personal choice

oils
In a spray can—to keep the fat at bay, but why buy aerosol? My daughter suggested buying a little plastic spritzer bottle, the kind you use for Evian water to spray your face on a dry airplane, or—slightly larger—to sprinkle clothes before ironing.[13] It works so well, I bought two: one for olive and one for vegetable oil.
- olive—different flavours, pepper, garlic, rosemary, etc.—buy them small and use them quickly.
- peanut—best for the wok, if you still use oil for cooking. Peanut oil has less odour and seems to me to be less flammable. (Olive oil doesn't take well to high heat.)
- sesame—essential for tahini and a delightful taste sensation in some salads.

13 *YOU STILL IRON??*

onions
° cooking—buy small bags and keep
  them at room temp.
° red—so good in so many things. Buy
  them singly.
° Spanish—I like Bermuda onions better.
  Buy them as you need them.
° garlic—clay jars work! Buy a braid only
  if you use garlic every single day.

pasta
See Pasta discussion on p. 182—too
many to mention here.

peanut butter
Some people can't live without it. I
can, but I'll tell you a quick dessert:
inch-long slices of banana spread with
a little chunky peanut butter. And failing all else for a swift bite for unexpected company, smash chunky peanut
butter into broad celery slices cut into
one-inch bites for a surprisingly edible
hors d'oeuvre.

peppers
Canned or bottled jalapeño—for adding
to kidney and other beans, including
refried, or to a tired cheese spread for
nachos.

raisins
Stir seedless ones into morning oatmeal, light cream cheese with cinnamon, evening curries, muesli, couscous,
on and on and on.[14]

14 *NEVER UNDERESTIMATE THE
POWER OF A RAISIN.*

Sauces

There are some wonderful bottled sauces in the market. Shop and taste around till you find one that suits your inner landscape. A few suggestions might include:

black bean with garlic

Devonshire custard—the canned stuff is amazingly good and useful for emergency dessert, with fresh or canned fruit and/or frozen pound cake

hoisin—nice on crêpes, to make your own Chinese roll-ups

Ketchup—Really? Why not use salsa instead? Yet I do still use the sloosh from a ketchup bottle: ½ cup (125 mL) *hot* water slooshed around in the heel and dregs. When you use it as seldom as I do, your heels and dregs need some persuading.

Szechuan—it is possible to make one's own (see p. 75) but only if you've run out

soy (Japanese)—look for salt-free or light

Tabasco—you know that joke about being able to tell how long a couple have been married by the number of bottles of Tabasco sauce they've used? I'm so old I've lost count. I wish I could still get sherry pepper sauce for Bloody Marys, but Tabasco will have to do.

taco sauce—a little package usually comes in your taco kit. Throw it onto your next pizza shell.

tahini—when did I discover sesame
and why not sooner?

For those who may have been lured into buying a
large bottle of tahini and don't know what to do with
it after they've made all the hummus they can eat,
consider the following uses of tahini:

Tahini on broccoli: Blend ¼ cup (50 mL) tahini
with 2 tbsp (25 mL) water, 1 clove garlic, 2 tbsp
(25 mL) lemon juice and a dollop of yogurt or sour
cream. Season with a grind or two of black pepper.
Pour over cooked broccoli (or not).

Tahini on carrots: Thin a little tahini with liquid
honey and toss with cooked baby carrots.

Tahini and spinach: Thin ¼ cup (50 mL) tahini
with 1 tbsp (15 mL) lemon juice and heat in a pan
with 1 tbsp (15 mL) sesame oil (or veg oil) and a
chopped garlic clove. Trim, wash and spin a bag of
spinach and toss it in the tahini mixture, coating
and cooking over high heat—about 4 or 5 minutes.

Tahini on rice: Blend 2 tbsp (25 mL) tahini with
1 tbsp (15 mL) soy sauce, the zest of an orange and a
little orange juice if it's too thick. Pour over cooked
rice.

Tahini Dressing: Blend ¼ cup (50 mL) of tahini,
1 tbsp (15 mL) lemon juice, 1 tbsp (15 mL) sesame
oil (or vegetable oil) and 1 mashed garlic clove.

Another Tahini Dressing: 2 oranges, peeled, 2 tbsp
(25 mL) tahini, 2 tsp (10 mL) liquid honey, 1 tsp
(5 mL) soy sauce, 1 tsp (5 mL) sesame oil (or veg).
Blend in your mini-processor. Use on spinach salad
or in Japanese Quinoa Salad (see p. 200).

Tahini Sandwich Spread: Blend ¼ cup (50 mL) peanut butter with 2 tbsp (25 mL) tahini. Moisten with lemon juice to desired spreadable consistency. Might be nice with pita bread and avocado and orange slices.

tamari—the concentrated soyest sauce we ever tasted, a well-kept secret of vegetarians until just recently[15]

teriyaki—light, or low-salt—good for a low-fat marinade for (skinned) chicken breasts before broiling

Worcestershire—one of the oldest and still one of the most useful. Don't forget to dash a little Wooster into your scrambled eggs.

Seasonings

basil, preferably fresh, but it doesn't hurt to have dried on the shelf

bay leaves—for soups and stews and barley and so on[16]

capers—for steak tartare and salads, especially Niçoise

caraway seeds—for cabbage and biscuits and salads (and breads)

chili peppers—for chili and guacamole and lots more

cinnamon—Shake some into the coffee before the boiling water goes on for an inexpensive flavoured coffee; mush it into (light) cream cheese with raisins to spread on your morning bagel; mix it with sugar and butter for teatime toast for unexpected guests, like your mother.

15 BY THE WAY, A TABLESPOON OF ANY PIQUANT SAUCE, THINNED WITH A DRIB OF OIL, SPIKED WITH A SMALL CHOPPED ONION, AND HEATED, IS A NICE COVER-UP FOR ALMOST ANY COOKED VEGETABLE.

16 I FORGOT, YOU DON'T COOK STUFF LIKE THAT.

coriander[17] —fresh, for soups, stews, couscous, pesto (p. 186)

cumin (seeds or ground)—for make-your-own curry, and fish soup and guacamole

curry powder—Yes!!! To release the full flavour of curry, you should heat it. Start it with the onions in butter, oil or chicken stock, and give it a chance. If it's going in a cold dish, like yogurt or sour cream for a dip, use more.

dillweed/seed—not interchangeable. The seed is good, well crushed to release the flavour, in beans, fish chowder, potato salad, coleslaw. Dillweed goes wonderfully well with salmon and shrimp, bean salad in a quick biscuit bread, and is to die for in a dill butter. (p. 139)

marjoram[18]

mustard, dry (the wet stuff is in the fridge)—dry is best for vinaigrette and to mix with beer and brown sugar to spread on a piece of back bacon to roast for brunch guests, or a baked canned luncheon meat for you (dinner and left-over sandwiches)

nutmeg, whole (with a nutmeg grater)—good on custard, bread pudding and instead of cinnamon on tea-toast

oregano—the best for pizza and spaghetti sauce, and for Greek salad. Marinate your olives in oil and oregano (dried or fresh).

pepper—black, whole and freshly ground. Reach for the pepper rather than for the salt. Wonderful on fresh sliced

17 YOU'RE PROBABLY WORRIED ABOUT HOW TO KEEP AND STORE FRESH HERBS LIKE BASIL, CORIANDER, WATERCRESS, PARSLEY AND SO ON. IF YOU CAN HELP IT, DON'T. BETTER TO DEAL WITH EACH OF THEM AND MAKE SOMETHING OF THEM. IF YOU HAVE TO, LOOSELY WRAP THE HERB IN QUESTION IN A GENEROUS SWATHE OF PAPER TOWELLING, SEAL IT IN A PLASTIC BAG AND FREEZE IT. BE SURE TO LABEL IT BECAUSE THEY ALL LOOK LIKE FESTERING WEEDS WHEN YOU TAKE THEM OUT TO USE THEM—FOR SOUPS AND PESTOS AND SPREADS. BETTER TO USE THEM WHEN THEY'RE FRESH AND FREEZE THE PRODUCTS. THE SPREADS AND DIPS AND PESTOS KEEP BETTER AND THEN YOU HAVE SOMETHING TANGIBLE TO FALL BACK ON.

18 I USED TO USE THIS WHEN I COOKED OXTAILS, BUT I HAVEN'T COOKED OXTAILS FOR YEARS. OXTAILS USED TO BE INEXPENSIVE, BUT AS WITH ALL OTHER RED MEAT, THE PRICE HAS SOARED. SIGH.

tomatoes, poached eggs, and in Greek and Caesar salads.

poppy seeds—try poppy seed butter on bread instead of garlic butter, prepared the same way. Poppy seeds mixed with honey make a wonderful spread for tea-toast.

rosemary—for one dish that's worth the price of admission, see Company Turkey, p. 213.

salt—the low-sodium kind. Even so, go easy.

salt-free mixes: with lemon, black pepper, your own mix

sesame seeds—wonderful! Be careful toasting sesame seeds as they burn awfully fast and I haven't figured out what to do with burnt ones.

sundried tomatoes—I don't like them, so you won't find them in my recipes. (It's *my* cookbook.)

sunflower seeds—the poor man's pine nut. Sprinkle them in salads, especially carrot and raisin; chop them for toppings and for cheese logs; try them in pestos; sprinkle in your oatmeal.

tarragon—especially wonderful with mushrooms and potatoes, but excellent in salads, especially the new designer greens

Check the dates on your spice and herb bottles, for goodness' sake! The contents lose strength as they age, so taste and toss if necessary, or increase the amount.

thyme—it used to be a stand-by with pork, often neglected now because people insist on using old, dried supplies and don't like the results

vanilla—the bean is nice; stick an inch (2.5 cm) in the sugar bowl. One bakes so little now, a bottle of real (not artificial) vanilla lasts a long time. Drop a little in milk to warm in the microwave if you can't sleep. Takes the baby-bottle stigma away and works with the lactose as an effective sedative, less addictive than OTC remedies. (Or try rum instead.)

watercress—see watercress butter, p. 138.

soups, dry, packaged
° instant, with noodles (stir in 1 tbsp/ 15 mL pesto)
° onion
° mix, to boil with stock—or not

sugar
° brown—for oatmeal, if you don't have maple syrup. To keep brown sugar from going hard, or if it already is, tear up a piece of fresh bread and drop into the bag or cannister.
° icing—on occasion, special that is
° white—don't forget the vanilla bean in your sugar bowl[19]

syrups
° apple, sugarless—good for oatmeal, or a baked apple (4 minutes in the microwave)

19 BECAUSE IT SMELLS GOOD AND TASTES NICE. PEOPLE WHO TAKE SUGAR THINK THEY'RE GETTING DESIGNER COFFEE.

° corn—for pancakes and corn bread and polenta (mush)
° maple—for pancakes, oatmeal, back bacon or ham, or in a can of beans.
° maple, light, imitation—cheaper, fewer calories, good for cooking oatmeal, (substitute ½ the water with syrup) but if you're indulging in pancakes, why not go whole hog and enjoy real maple slurp?

taco shells

If you have too many left over from a taco supper, break them into chips and serve them with a dip or zap them with cheese and serve hot like nachos.

tomatoes, canned, juice, paste and soup. Stand-bys, as necessary.

vinegars
° apple cider—a vinegar with conviction, taken in homeopathic doses in a variety of home remedies, for treating diets, coughs and ulcers. Cheaper than balsamic with lots of zing, and delightful mixed with honey as a quick fruit salad dressing
° balsamic—expensive, but delicious; good with meats
° raspberry—for warm chicken salad and the like[20]
° red or white wine, seasoned, specialty
° regular or white (it's a basic, and you can clean your coffeemaker with it by running it with a mixture of white vinegar and water)

20 WHEN I WAS A LITTLE GIRL MY GRANDMOTHER USED TO MAKE WHAT SHE CALLED RASPBERRY VINEGAR AND CONCOCTED A COOL DRINK WITH IT LIKE LEMON-ADE (AN INCH OR SO OR OF THE VINEGAR IN THE BOTTOM OF THE GLASS, TOPPED WITH WATER)—A FAR CRY FROM THE TART LIQUID PEOPLE TOSS ON THE BITTER GREENS TODAY. IS THIS PROGRESS?

° rice wine—my favourite. I don't need dressing if I have rice wine to pour on my salad.

But here, if you must, is the alternative:

VINAIGRETTE FOR ONE

¼ cup (50 mL) olive oil, or less

2 tbsp (25 mL) lemon juice

a couple of grinds of black pepper

salt to taste (go easy)

¼ tsp (1 mL) dry mustard

Whip the ingredients in a measuring cup with a fork, making sure the mustard is mixed in, or, easier, pour into a small jar with a tight-fitting lid and shake it up. Anything left over keeps in the jar in the fridge. Pour at your discretion over a salad and toss it with abandon. Remember the Spanish proverb about the requisites for a perfect salad: "Let the salad-maker be a spendthrift for oil, a miser for vinegar, a statesman for salt, and a madman for mixing."

Drop a little white vinegar into your water when poaching an egg to keep the white from messing up.

water chestnuts—Good in spinach salads

Now for the cold stuff, but by the way, just to reassure you: I do not have a huge upright or even a small chest freezer. I have a small fridge with a freezer compartment across the top with a separate door. Anything I suggest you freeze has been tested not only for my freezer but also for limited storage capacity. An expert's list for what you should have on hand in the freezer is not only unrealistic, it's expensive. Even though you don't earn interest on the money invested in food in your freezer, these are still frozen assets. Stock what you think is practical and use it within a reasonable time. Six months is usually the outside time you can store anything in the freezer, and cooked foods must be used sooner than that. We've already mentioned the siege mentality. Be prepared, by all means, but don't be freezer-poor.

FROZEN ASSETS

breads
° 6 bagels
° 1 basic loaf, sliced (whole wheat or multi-grain)
° 6 English muffins (alternate with bagels if you're crowded)
° 1 garlic bread[21]

21 IF YOU HAVE FRENCH BREAD LEFT OVER, SLICE IT, SPREAD IT WITH GARLIC BUTTER, WRAP IT IN FOIL AND FREEZE IT. YOU'LL BE SO GRATEFUL TO YOURSELF!

Cooked stuff: keep a running inventory. Most cooked food should be used within 6 weeks.

eggs
° Egg Beaters, or not
° egg whites, an accumulation

fish
° 1 package of fillets
° 1 package of pollock (cut-up imitation crabmeat)

Ice cream, or frozen yogurt, or sherbet (lighter choices). Buy for company or deep depression, but not too much.

juice concentrates
° apple (see Bran Muffins, p. 110)
° orange
° grapefruit

and for summer

° lemonade—I prefer a daiquiri mix
  myself, or
° piña colada mix

meat
° chicken, ground, made into patties
  (with two layers of waxed paper between
  each one)
° turkey breast—takes up space, but grab
  it when you can
° turkey, cooked, ground, made into
  patties

nuts
° pecan
° pine

seasonings
° fresh ginger

soup, in cubes and containers

tomato paste, frozen in tablespoon-
sized (15 mL) blobs and bagged for
doling

vegetables
° mix for emergency primavera or beef stew
° duxelles: cooked, chopped mushrooms
  frozen in cubes or blobs
° peas for sprained ankles
° others at your discretion
° bags of tops of celery and such, for
  stock

Now let us furnish a hypothetical fridge.

IN THE FRIDGE

butter, well-wrapped because you don't use it much and you don't want it to pick up memories of other foods

cheese, preferably low-fat
° cottage cheese, also low-fat
° cream cheese, light[22]

eggs (buy six at a time)

greens and veggies, fresh

ditto **fruit**, but most is better at room temp. A whole orange (or a half grapefruit) is better for you than juice—more fibre, more calcium, more filling.

juice—not for me!

leftovers (see Chapter 5)[23]

lemons and/or lemon juice

limes

mayonnaise—light

milk, buttermilk

salad dressings

salsa, commercial (you could make your own, but why?)

yogurt, low-fat

22 EVEN LIGHT SHOULD BE ONLY AN OCCASIONAL GUEST.

23 LEFTOVERS ARE THE BASE NOTE OF ANY FRIDGE. YOU CAN QUOTE ME ON THAT.

There! All stocked up and the world is your oyster, if you like oysters. You're the one who decides. What do you want to eat?

CHAPTER FIVE

Leftovers

> *There are people who don't like leftovers*
> *dealt with any old how and my advice to*
> *them is: get born into a large family.*
>
> ~ *Betty Jane Wylie*

One of the biggest challenges singles face in the kitchen is leftovers.[1] There's a good crossword puzzle word for them: orts. It comes from the Middle English, meaning morsels or scraps, deriving from the Old English *etan*, eat. Edible orts are a challenge.

Back in the days when I made house calls, that is, when I was promoting my leftovers cookbook, I became a fridge therapist. As my friends realized that I brought with me the skills to restore their fridges to sanity and sanitation, sorting out the contents, reconciling the disparate odds and ends of everyone's busy life, nowhere more evident than in their leftovers, and coming up with some edible, guilt-free food, they issued warm invitations for me

1 I'VE OFTEN WONDERED WHY PEOPLE DON'T TRADE LEFTOVERS IN THE SAME WAY THAT SOME WOMEN SWAP CHRISTMAS BAKING. I GUESS IT WOULD TAKE TOO MUCH ORGANIZING AND TIME TO DO IT ON A REGULAR BASIS. BESIDES, LEFTOVERS ARE PRETTY PERSONAL. I WOULDN'T WANT TO WALK IN ANOTHER WOMAN'S MOCCASINS AND I WOULDN'T WANT TO EAT ANOTHER PERSON'S LEFTOVERS. NOT THAT I HAVEN'T.

to come and visit. I was allowed, even welcomed, to muddle in other people's fridges and meddle with their gustatory habits. One is seldom allowed to do that with someone else's desk, or with a love life that needs tidying and recycling. Pity. A few of my hosts, of course, were adamant that their fridges remain private and uninspected. They scarcely allowed me to open the fridge door to get milk for my morning tea. I don't blame them a bit. Refrigerators are very intimate. We've already had that conversation.

Most singles will readily admit the presence of lurking leftovers. It is a fact of life that if you live alone, you will always have orts. Women are as vulnerable as men, but perhaps more ready to confess, repent and perform an act of attrition. Guilt-ridden creatures of either gender don't handle leftovers well. That's why I'm here. The sooner we acknowledge that leftovers are always with us, the sooner we can deal with them. These days using up your leftovers is called recycling, so it has an ethical appeal. By keeping your leftovers out of landfill you are not only saving money, you are also doing your bit for the planet.

Before I lay out a basic strategy for your leftovers, I would like to point out the difference between genuine leftovers, which are cooked, and an overabundance of something, which is usually raw, like too much of a vegetable you were forced to buy to get what you wanted, or which may be in a primitive state, like the rest of a can or bottle of something you had to open and use only a tablespoon of. In all cases, you must be vigilant. Constant vigilance is the only way to save your planet from pollution, your fridge from mould and your self from guilt, or boredom. To this end, I will set a few ground rules:

ORTFUL RULES

- ° It pays to plan ahead.
- ° Frying is not the answer.[2]
- ° Think laterally.
- ° Your best friend is your freezer.
- ° Never overestimate people's taste buds, that is,
- ° Maintain your respect for food and
- ° Don't throw good money after bad.[3]
- ° Know when to give up, throw it out and call take-out.

[2] THE FAMOUS FRENCH COOK BRILLAT-SAVARIN SAID, "FRYING GIVES COOKS NUMEROUS WAYS OF CONCEALING WHAT APPEARED THE DAY BEFORE." TIMES, I KEEP SAYING, CHANGE.

[3] IF YOU DIDN'T LIKE SOMETHING IN THE FIRST PLACE, CHANCES ARE YOU WON'T LIKE IT IN THE SEC-OND OR THIRD, NO MATTER HOW YOU DOCTOR IT.

In addition to the rules, you have to have a basic philosophy. My basics have changed over the years, as I'm sure yours have, if you've lived long enough. For instance, I no longer approve of high-fat solutions to low-grade problems. Heating leftover meat in a mess of old gravy or greasing up cooked potatoes in a well of hot bacon fat is not a healthy solution; it's going from the fire into the fat, not good. Ditto sugar. Coating something with chocolate or custard sauce, rolling something in icing sugar, chopping candy into ice cream or pouring melted ice cream over (chocolate) pasta or into eggnog or batter is high-rolling, not recycling, and costs too many calories.

I try to eat healthful food, not only bracing myself against decadent, dangerous temptation but also learning to prefer and enjoy food that is better for me. Before that makes me sound too prissy, I will say that everyone deserves a treat—regularly. All fibre and no fun makes Jill a stick. I also like to save money, or if not save, at least not waste it. I have a very low tolerance for waste. That's why I consider an aggressive use of leftovers so important. Storing something in a Petri dish at the back of the fridge until it develops penicillin and can righteously be tossed is not my idea of the creative use of leftovers.

When faced with a culinary conundrum—the question being, toss now or dump later—ask yourself, and answer honestly, "Do I care if I never see this again?"

Lastly, I consider leftovers to be one of the major challenges of the single life. I love challenges.

Now for some ortful application of the rules.

It pays to plan ahead

Grilled vegetables are popular now: wonderful assemblies of peppers, red onion, zucchini, eggplant, sometimes mushrooms, carrots and so on. It pays to cook too much because they have a wonderful after-life as leftovers, turning up happily on focaccia with grated Parmesan or Asiago cheese sprinkled on top and lightly broiled. They can be tossed gently into pasta for a second meal. If you don't want to see them again, throw them in soup, or in the freezer until your next shot at the stock pot.

Don't forget all the root vegetables and how full of beta-carotene and fibre they are. Lightly roasted ones—sweet potatoes, parsnips, carrots—keep well for several days in the fridge and can be reheated in the microwave with no loss of flavour, in fact they seem to me to get better as they relax and get to know each other.

I usually make enough salad for two or three meals because I find chopping before every meal to be tedious. I don't mind leftover salad because I never put dressing (just rice wine vinegar) on it in the first place, so it doesn't get soggy. You can pour off any liquid the greens have exuded before you eat it the second time, or store the salad in a large bowl in the bottom of which you have inverted a saucer. This way, the liquid collects underneath the salad, segregated from the veggies. If there's too much or if it gets soggy, dump it in your blender or processor with a cup of tomato juice and a dash of Worcestershire sauce and whirl it—briefly!—into a lumpy gazpacho, with maybe some new celery for extra crunch. Nice for a summer lunch with a few croutons sprinkled on top.[4]

An overabundance of pasta without any sauce is easy to deal with. Rinsed in cold water and tossed in a smidge of oil, it will keep in the fridge to be used within a couple of days, or you can freeze it in a tub of water and thaw it later by quick immersion into boiling water. It can also be frozen mixed into sauce, in which case bake it when you reincarnate it, crusted with cheese. I prefer individual servings because I can control the amount of food I serve myself. As for leftover cooked noodles, there's always a **quickie kugel:** tossing them with an egg beaten in a little yogurt and/or cottage cheese, smushing them into a flat ovenware dish and baking the pudding for half an hour at 350°F (180°C). Salty, with crumbs and grated cheese on top, and artistically strewn mushroom caps before you bake it, this is lunch or supper; sweet, with a little sugar in the egg mixture and a cinnamon topping, chilled after baking, and with fresh strawberries on top, it's delicious for breakfast instead of toast or cereal.

Frying is not the answer

I never have leftover mashed potatoes any more because I don't serve myself or anyone mashed potatoes—all that cream and butter!—but I do often

4 YEARS AGO WHEN I WAS PROMOTING MY LEFTOVERS COOKBOOK, I APPEARED LIVE ON THE OLD **BOB MCLEAN SHOW** ON CBC. I TOOK MY OWN CUISINART, VERY NEW THEN, AND INGREDIENTS, AND SET UP MY MATERIAL ON A COUNTER, BEING CAREFUL TO CHECK THE ELECTRICAL OUTLET. LATER, I NOTICED A CREW MEMBER ALSO FIDDLING WITH IT BUT THOUGHT NO MORE ABOUT IT UNTIL I WAS ON, DOING MY GAZPACHO NUMBER. I DUMPED THE SALAD INTO THE PROCESSOR, ADDED A FEW SEASONINGS, POURED IN A GENEROUS SLOSH OF TOMATO JUICE AND TURNED THE MOTOR ON. NOTHING HAPPENED.

"AND THERE YOU HAVE," I SAID TO BOB, "A VERY SOGGY SALAD!" WE LAUGHED AND AD LIBBED WHILE THE ELECTRICIAN CRAWLED ALONG THE FLOOR TO PLUG IN THE APPLIANCE AGAIN. THIS IS NOT TO ILLUSTRATE THE JOY OF COOKING, THIS IS TO SHOW YOU THE JOY OF LIVE TELEVISION. TRUST ME, THE GAZPACHO IS TERRIFIC.

deliberately have leftover boiled ones—both mini and new. Tiny ones, barely cooked, sprinkled with fresh dill, make a great nibble before dinner—less fat than peanuts—but you could also zap them with a little (or a lot of) chopped garlic in a spritz of oil. Larger leftover potatoes become **potato salad** dressed with ½ cup (125 mL) light yogurt instead of sour cream, mixed with 1 tbsp (15 mL) of light mayo, lots of crushed dill seeds and tons of chopped celery for crunch, and that's the only potato salad recipe you'll get from me.

Other leftover vegetables, if cooked crisp enough the first time that they won't fall apart with the pressure of a second appearance, easily become the ingredients of a **pasta primavera stir-fry**—pretty with penne or fusilli (see p. 187). These include broccoli, cauliflower, green beans and peppers, both red and green, although these are better to add fresh for zing and crunch. Leftover vegetables are also good in frittatas: eggplant, zucchini, fresh mushrooms, and so on (see p. 142).[5]

5 *FRITTATA DESERVES A PHILOSO-PHY OF ITS OWN; IT'S QUICHE WITHOUT THE PASTRY AND REAL MEN EAT IT.*

Think laterally

Where I live now one cannot choose the amount or the age of feta cheese one buys. The first time I had an excess from a Greek salad, the feta was going dry on me. In desperation I dumped it in my mini-processor with several cloves of garlic and chopped it all together into potent crumbles. Now I do it deliberately. The **Feta-Garlic Crumbles** keep well in the fridge and sprinkle beautifully on hot spinach, heated in the microwave to melt the cheese. If you want more bulk than that, spread the spinach (drained well) on an individual ready-to-bake pizza round, sprinkle with the Crumbles and bake at

400°F (200°C) for 5 or 6 minutes. Or put it on pita bread or a piece of toast and zap it in the microwave. It's called lunch.

Chopped leftover cold cuts, which I have seldom bought since my vegetarian daughter offered me a "nitrite sandwich," or sliced pepperoni can become part of a pizza topping.

Too much leftover cheese, after a holiday wine and cheese party, can present a problem, the problem being how to eat it before it all goes *bleu*. I recently had a lot of leftover cheese and rather than making a cheese spread as I would have done in MOL, I made a cheese fondue for my grandchildren, melting and blending the grated cheese with white wine and serving it with lots of raw vegetables as well as some crusty bread. Any sauce you might have left over from such a solution you could dribble sparingly over hot spinach for lunch, or pour over a split baked potato for dinner—and that's all. I mean, no meat—but you could have a salad.

Your best friend is your freezer

Yes, you can freeze a banana, in its skin. A frozen banana can be eaten with a spoon and tastes like ice cream but it's much lower fat. In My Other Life, I used to make banana cake. If you like it, bake cupcakes instead of a layer or slab, and freeze them for one-shot indulgences. Banana in the bran muffin batter is delicious and muffins make good breakfasts, one at a time. If you're too busy to bake banana muffins today, freeze the banana mush and resurrect it within four weeks.

Leftover rice doesn't freeze too well by itself, but you can mix it with kidney beans as the base of a vegetarian chili. Or immerse it in a well of stock and it will be fine as in soup when it re-emerges, or in a casserole with other leftovers who need a friend. Don't try to thaw it to serve alone because the texture is grainy; better to make it into stir-fried rice (Chicken, p. 159; Mushroom, p. 195).

At my local, only grocery store last fall I inquired wistfully about spaghetti squash and then felt honour-bound, when the produce manager brought in 12 (the minimum he had to purchase), to use as many as I could. One spaghetti squash goes a long way for a single consumer; three last forever. Well, at least until July. I discovered I could freeze half a squash, wrapped, but it took up a lot of room. So I cooked the next one and scraped out the "spaghetti" and froze that, both in large amounts in a freezer package and already sauced in my ever-ready serving dishes.[6]

I seldom have stale or mouldy bread because I keep my bread in the freezer and use it by the slice as I need it. But if you have a couple of slices of bread you want to get rid of, spread them with garlic or herb butter and broil or heat them for dinner, or with butter and cinnamon sugar, heated, for breakfast or tea, or grind them into bread crumbs.[7]

Don't throw good money after bad

I can't decide which is my worst problem with leftovers: having to leave town or coping with the aftermath of company when I have only one mouth to give.[8] I mean, there is all that food. It's obvious that each situation requires different treatment. I call it situational ethics in the kitchen, and here's a Wylie Rule I forgot to mention: The prime rule of a leftover cook is *improvise*, also, *experiment*.

Rather than make a unilateral decision by tossing without testing, I've experimented a lot, to discover

6 *I THINK I'LL PASS ON THE SQUASH FOR A WHILE AND I WON'T EVER BE WISTFUL IN THE PRODUCE DEPARTMENT AGAIN.*

7 *IF YOU STILL HAVE BREAD TO USE, AFTER YOU'VE MADE FRENCH TOAST, CROUTONS, BREAD PUDDING AND CROSTINI, THEN COME AND FEED MY BIRDS AND SQUIRRELS.*

8 *YOU COULD, OF COURSE, HAVE TWO DINNER PARTIES BACK TO BACK, THEREBY HAVING TO CLEAN HOUSE ONLY ONCE AND USING UP ALL THE DESSERT.*

for myself what I can freeze and what I can't, finding out the hard way. Of course you can't freeze celery—well, yes, you can. In a bag, cut up, and drop it in the stock pot next time you make soup—just don't plan to use it in a salad. I also cut up tomatoes and freeze them and throw them in my next red pasta sauce. Leftover salsa goes into the freezer with the same goal,[9] and peppers, but not cucumber—it just goes mushy. But it will keep, swirled up with yogurt and dill and, okay, a little salt, as a dressing you'll use when you get home, if you're not gone too long.

I have a rich friend who lives in Bermuda. She was brought up frugal like me; our mothers knew how to make one dollar do the work of two and look like five. Big spending doesn't come naturally to her, especially in the kitchen. She makes **lettuce soup**. Rather than throw out tired, rusty lettuce, she turns it into the soup pot with anything else that comes to hand, boils it and then purées it. The colour is something else. Dishwater comes to mind. I recommend Kitchen Bouquet to make it look like soup and add zing. An old-fashioned product I was surprised to find is still in the market, Kitchen Bouquet is caramelized sugar with some dried spices and vegetables, designed to make meats and soups and stews look appetizing. A demi-glace would do it, too, but that takes days.

Improvise

Eggs present another problem to singles. These days you aren't supposed to eat more than four eggs a week max, although the "Get Cracking" people are trying to say something about that. Even if you ask the store clerk to cut a carton in half for you, you still have six to work on. You can freeze whites easily

9 CONTRARY TO POPULAR OPINION, SALSA CAN GO BAD AND DEVELOP MOULD ON THE SURFACE. SAVE IT FROM ITSELF BY POPPING IT IN THE FREEZER BEFORE YOU GO AWAY.

and cumulatively, adding layers to the container already in the freezer, and make an angel food cake for a treat for company when you have a cup and a half's worth, no problem there. Egg whites will keep up to 6 months in the freezer. You can also make a frittata with four to six eggs. When it's cooked and cooled, cut it into serving-sized pieces, wrap and freeze them for individual lunch servings if you eat at home (or zap it at the office?), or a quick light supper, with lots of hot salsa and fruit.

You cannot so easily drop an extra egg into a nog or a mayonnaise these days, because of the fear of salmonella. Don't forget to coddle yourself by coddling the egg before you use it. (See p. 3.)

Fresh herbs are not available where I live, so I have to import them from the big city. I can romp through a bunch of basil without a thought, but watercress and cilantro and dill often spoil before I can use up the family-size bunches I have to buy. I started improvising pestos and butters with them and they keep beautifully, and freeze well, if need be. (See pesto, p. 184.)

Sooner or later, I knew we'd have to deal with the improvisational leader in the kitchen: the casserole. As I've told you, I was the Casserole Queen of the '50s. I developed a method I called Compose-a-Casserole, by which related foods were teamed up to play again another day. I used to think it was hard sometimes, trying to feed six of us with a leftover dib of this and a tired dab of that, brought to you courtesy of mushroom soup and don't talk about the clichéd toppings. I was wrong. It's harder to cut down, to feed without stuffing or boring one lone consumer who is going to scream if she has to open another can of mushroom soup.

Too fat, anyway. Think chicken stock instead. Think stir-fry. Think fusilli and peppers, red and green, think elegant morsels of delectable orts. And if you're totally at a loss, think finger foods and forget all about casseroles. You'll see what I mean when you read the recipe for Chicken Divan on p. 152 — no soup. Forget soup.

Maintain your respect for food

A TORTILLA IN THE HAND, also known as **FAJITAS**

Take one or two soft tortillas and build some-thing. Spread the surface with hoisin sauce or Szechuan or even ketchup. Now take a little chopped cooked meat (turkey? chicken?) and sprin-kle it over the sauce. Add your choice and combina-tion of chopped green pepper, tomato and avocado, and grated cheese. Roll up tightly, put seam side down in a microwave dish and zap until oozing and delicious. Eat with a bib.

One of the easiest, favourite things I serve to grandchildren or a crowd is make-your-own tacos (p. 217), with a variety of choices, thus suiting the vegetarians in our family's midst. Here's what I do with the leftovers:

LEFTOVER TACOS

The leftover lettuce goes into the next day's salad, along with the guacamole as part of the dressing thinned with a little lemon juice. The chopped tomatoes and peppers along with the grated cheese and salsa — if there's not too much — all get mixed in with the leftover hamburger and popped into a casserole with a cup of cooked macaroni for the freezer, and maybe a can of niblet corn if it looks skimpy. This casserole might serve two as an informal instant dinner with a salad, garlic bread, a bottle of Chianti and a friend, or if it's just me, I divide it into two or more individual servings.

Turkey is a popular year-round offering now, easy for a single to serve to a small crowd.[10] The leftovers are not difficult to cope with. Take the meat off the carcass and chop it up, slice it, dice it, grind it,[11] then turn the bones into the soup pot. Package the cooked meat in varying amounts, wrapping it well in both clear wrap and foil. Shape the ground meat at once into individual patties (see p. 162) and freeze them between double layers of freezer or waxed paper so that you can thaw one at a time for yourself. The rest of the meat will make fajitas, divan, stir-fries, on and on. The same goes for chicken.

For the big-meat eaters among you, keep in mind that a leftover lamb roast becomes a quick curry and the meaty bone is the basis of Scotch broth. Leftover beef leaves you with hot beef sandwiches with gravy, shepherd's pie, Beef Roll-Ups (p. 77) and Devilled Beef Bones (p. 176), if you're lucky.

I think it's time to have an elementary discussion of soup. Never mind the *Larousse Dictionary of Food*, which goes on and on about soups for 22½ pages, two columns to a page. We are not gourmet cooks, you and I; we are survivors. All we have to know is the difference between stock and soup and how to get from one to the other. Stock is the liquid in which meat or fish or vegetables have been cooked, the basis for soups and sauces and in my case for stir-fry. Soup is the liquid food that results

10 *YES, EASY. RUB A TEASPOON OF SALT IN THE CAVITY OF AN 8-TO 10-LB TURKEY, DROP IN A WHOLE PEELED ONION, MASSAGE THE BIRD LIGHTLY WITH A TEASPOON OF OIL, AND ROAST IT AT 325°F (160°C) FOR 3 TO 3½ HOURS. THAT'S IT, NO STUFFING, NO GRAVY. IN THE SUMMER YOU DON'T EVEN NEED HOT VEGETABLES. PUT OUT A PLATTER OF LETTUCE, TOMATOES, RED ONIONS AND SUCH AND SOME GOOD BREAD AND LET PEOPLE MAKE THEIR OWN HOT TURKEY SANDWICHES.*

11 *IN YOUR MINI-CHOPPER, IF IT'S NOT MORE THAN TWO OR THREE PATTIES' WORTH.*

from adding good stuff to stock. A good soup requires a history, not a recipe. Good stock is as near as your leftovers. The method is always the same; the taste will vary with your ingredients.

The only trouble with soup and the single cook is that there's too much of it and too few of you. Even your freezer is going to protest. So have some friends for lunch. Or give a jar of it to a sick neighbour. Good soup makes good neighbours.[12]

BASIC STOCK

Clear out your freezer: drop in the contents of all the little bags of celery tops and cuttings you've been saving for the last couple of months. Add a couple of scraped carrots, a large onion, quartered, and whatever bones you have accumulated. If you're making chicken or turkey stock, obviously you should have chicken or turkey bones. Use a turkey carcass; or a small utility or boiling fowl, and use the meat in à la king, dropping the shreds back in the stock. If you've had chicken wings, I hope you cut off the wing tips to freeze and add to this stock because they'll make it jell. If you have a lamb bone from a roast with plenty of meat clinging to it, fine, ditto roast beef.

But whom are we kidding? How often do you have big meat? So go to the meat counter and buy one or two packages of soup bones and dump them in the pot. Fill the pot with water, add a palm-full of salt (about 1 tbsp/15 mL), 6 or 8 whole peppercorns and 1 or 2 bay leaves. Bring to a boil, skim off any froth that forms, lower the heat and leave on a strong simmer for several hours or until the place smells like a boarding house. Strain, cool, skim off the fat and then decide what you're going to do.

These days, if it's chicken stock, no problem. I freeze it in ice cube trays and package the cubes in plastic bags. One or two cubes gives me my cooking liquid for stir-fry, eggplant, peppers, all kinds of things that used to soak up oil.

If it's lamb stock, then you must cook barley, long-cooking as it is,[13] and when it's tender, add it to the liquid along with fresh-cut carrot coins, diced celery and onion. If it's beef stock, enjoy the marrow[14] and add other things: rice or noodles or spaghettini broken into inch-long pieces, and other good tastes, including a goodly dollop of coriander pesto (p. 186), which does amazing things to soup. I learned that in Ecuador, and this: drop in inch-long pieces of leftover cooked corn *on* the cob. Cook the soup gently until the new inhabitants feel at home—about 5 minutes—and serve.

I am now working on what to do with too much hummus. One can of chick peas goes a long way, especially without guests. One freezing is okay, not two. I'll be glad to ship my leftover hummus to whoever wants it, collect. In the meantime, I'm freezing it in smaller containers so I won't thaw it all the next time.

Here's one dish I've developed, treating the hummus like polenta.

13 THE MINUTE I BEGAN DISCUSSING SOUP I BROKE MY FIVE-MINUTE RULE, ANYWAY. HOW TO COOK *BARLEY*: BOIL FOR AN HOUR IN 1/2 TO 1-1/2 CUPS (125 TO 375 ML) OF WATER OR STOCK WITH A TEASPOON OR LESS OF SALT AND A QUARTERED ONION. WHEN TENDER, IT WILL HAVE ABSORBED MOST OF THE LIQUID. YOU NOW HAVE SEVERAL OPTIONS, SOUP BEING THE SIMPLEST ONE.

14 HOT BONE MARROW ON TOAST WITH SALT IS A RICH (FAT) TREAT. IT USED TO BE SO POPULAR THE BONES WERE SERVED WRAPPED IN LITTLE NAPKINS, WITH SPECIAL BONE MARROW SPOONS.

HUMMUS AND MUSHROOMS

1 fistful of hummus (p. 68)

1 small onion, thinly sliced

6 to 8 medium mushrooms, sliced

1 tsp (5 mL) oil (sesame would be nice)

2 thumb-and-forefinger pinches of dried thyme

2 fierce grinds of black pepper

a generous snipping of parsley or coriander

Thaw your hummus and spread it on a plate in a pleasing circle with an indentation in the middle. Sauté the onions and mushrooms in the oil until the onions are friendly and the mushrooms have stopped being self-conscious, about 2 minutes. Stir in the seasonings, quickly bringing them to heel, about 1 minute, and spoon the mixture into the centre of the hummus. Scoop with warm pita bread.

It may seem odd to run the leftovers ahead of the main attractions, but singles, both young and old, know that anything is easy the first time around. It's how you deal with the consequences that reveals your competence and maturity. Anyone can open a can or a package or dial a number for take-out. Not everyone can look in a lonely but crowded fridge and come up with an inexpensive, swift, delicious, comforting solution to the ubiquitous problem: what is there to eat?

As a matter of fact, I know one smart single who *buys* leftovers. When he orders take-out he often has to round out his order anyway to reach the minimum expenditure required for delivery. If he's ordering Chinese, he asks for an extra serving of rice, plain steamed or fried; with chicken he orders the extra serving required (all the bones for soup; wings with hot salsa the next night); anyone knows what to do with leftover pizza.[15]

This may well be the chapter you refer to most often, the practical approach to a never-ending quandary. My brother used to say of my mother's leftovers that he wished he had been around when the original meal was served. Singles tend to feel like that, too, only more so, since you can remember being there for the original and you're *still* there. Take heart. Nothing lasts forever, not even leftovers. You could always start a compost heap.

CHAPTER SIX

Breakfast

To boil an egg, my darling daughter—
Put it in cold and not hot water.

~ Mary Hosford

"**B**reakfast like a king," the saying goes, "lunch like a prince, and dine like a pauper."[1] In female terms, this would read: queen, princess and bag lady. It means, of course, that you should take the bulk of your calories early so as to burn them off during the day. Stoke your furnace in the morning, then bank your coals at night. It makes sense, but no one does it these days. Our schedules don't permit it.

We used to be a rural society, dependent on the land for our livelihood and tied to it for our work. Farm eating habits were diametrically opposed to present-day big-city ways. Huge breakfasts were consumed at five in the morning, after the cows were milked and the appetite had kicked in, all this food

1 I LOOKED AROUND AND
    DISCOVERED THAT THE LATE
    AMERICAN FOOD GURU ADELLE
    DAVIS SAID THIS.

to stoke the body for the man-killing work of the day. Woman-killing, too, because someone had to cook it all, and dinner too (at noon). The evening meal was light, often cold, and bedtime was early.

No more. People are too urban, too busy, too sleepy or too pressured to make and eat breakfast. Besides, they don't feel like it. Hard enough to gird one's loins for the new day without having to eat first. The basic bugaboos of breakfast are basal metabolism and boredom.[2] It is not the role of this cookbook to rearrange singles' lives and metabolisms with cute little eggnogs (beware the frumious salmonella in raw eggs) or brown bag breakfasts. To paraphrase Yogi Berra's line, if people aren't going to eat breakfast, you can't stop them.

You can't take any basics for granted any more, especially when it comes to breakfast. Breakfasts are very personal. Ask people what they have for breakfast and you get an enthusiastic, elaborate answer about very little, or else more information than you care to know about someone's metabolism or personal life that precludes all thoughts of eating anything in the morning. So why am I giving you this chapter? I suppose because I have a messianic complex: whatever I undertake I want to hold the torch, lead others along the path, and light the fire to cook by. If the path leads to breakfast, so be it. Somewhere in this assortment of advice a breakfast boycotter might find an answer, not having known there was a question. Already committed breakfast eaters may find a new idea, or maybe just an idea they needed to be reminded of.

Just to remind you: don't forget Canada's Food Guide. If you're going to manage to consume 5 to 10 fruits and vegetables a day, you're going to have

2   SINGLES THINK PARENTS HAVE AN ADVANTAGE BECAUSE THEY HAVE TO COOK AND SET A GOOD EXAMPLE FOR THE KIDS. THIS IS NOT A GIVEN. MOST PEOPLE, FAMILIES INCLUDED, MOVE IN A VACUUM IN THE MORNING. I COULD WRITE A SONG: "ONE BOWL, ONE SPOON, WE'LL TALK AT NOON."

to start early with at least one selection at breakfast. Then think dairy, think fibre, think protein (a small amount), well, actually, don't think. Find something that will get you through the morning and stick with it. People may like variety at night but rigid routine in the morning helps to define the new day.[3]

So.

Did anyone say anything about your morning shot of vitamin C? More effective in food than in a pill.[4] And more effective in a whole fruit than in juice, because you get fibre and calcium too. You may not have time to sit down to eat half a grapefruit but you could take a whole orange with you and eat it at your coffee break.

There's not much to say about cold cereal. I note that the cereal people are pushing it for times other than breakfast. Among the people I interviewed this has already happened: they eat cereal as a snack before bed, or sometimes for dessert. Only one I talked to ate it for dinner, but I have read that this is a growing trend among the non-cooking singles; what's more, they eat it in bed. We take a variety of cereals for granted since Kellogg swept the nation with nature's broom, but the best ones really are a good source of protein (with milk) and fibre, too. Read the list of ingredients, and if sugar is the first one, put the box back on the shelf.

Yogurt, fruited or not, sprinkled with bran or not, with or without muesli, (p. 145) ditto honey, gets a lot of votes these days among the more health-conscious singles. Low-fat, of course. Some people make their own low-fat, low-sugar bran muffins, ignoring the high-calorie brown cake that passes for a bran muffin in the breakfast vans and coffee shops.

3 IF YOU DON'T BELIEVE ME, WATCH ANYONE AT BREAKFAST IN A HOTEL DINING ROOM. THE KEY WORD IS RITUAL, ALSO KNOWN AS HABIT.

4 SPEAKING OF WHICH, VITAMINS AND MINERALS AREN'T ABSORBED VERY WELL UNLESS THEY'RE TAKEN WITH FOOD. SO DON'T THINK THAT A GLASS OF WATER OR A CUP OF COFFEE AND A MULTI-VITAMIN PILL WILL SUFFICE.

HEALTHY BRAN MUFFINS

1½ cups (375 mL) bran cereal

1 cup (250 mL) raisins

¼ cup (50 mL) vegetable oil

½ cup (125 mL) frozen apple juice concentrate

1¼ cups (300 mL) whole wheat flour

1¼ tsp (6 mL) baking soda

¼ tsp (1 mL) salt

1 egg, beaten

1 cup (250 mL) buttermilk

2 tbsp (25 mL) liquid honey

Dump the bran cereal, raisins and oil into a large bowl. Heat the apple juice concentrate to boiling and pour it over the mixture, stirring to moisten. Blend the flour, baking soda and salt and dump it in with the cereal. Combine the egg, buttermilk and honey and pour this wet mixture into the viscous stuff, stirring just enough to moisten everything. If you can spare the time, cover the batter, stow it in the fridge and let it bubble[5] a while. Fill the greased cups of a muffin pan and don't worry about over-flow—no one does these days. Bake at 400°F (200°C) for 20 to 25 minutes. Let them cool 5 or 10 minutes in the pan then carefully remove, and cool completely on a rack. Makes 12 muffins.

5 *IT DOESN'T **RISE** BECAUSE THERE'S NO YEAST IN IT, BUT THE BAKING SODA **LIFTS** IT AND IT DOESN'T HURT FOR THE INGREDIENTS TO GET TO KNOW EACH OTHER A LITTLE BETTER.*

Return the unused portion of concentrate to the freezer for the next bran muffin seizure, or else make it up and drink it. As for the buttermilk, pour 1 cup (250 mL) over fish to cook in the microwave. Stir into your dairy mixture for kugel (p. 95), whirl in the processor with cooked cauliflower & curry for a cold summer soup, or make buttermilk pancakes for Sunday brunch.

Here's another nice muffin mix:

CORN MUFFINS

1 cup (250 mL) cornmeal

1 cup (250 mL) whole wheat flour

4 tsp (20 mL) baking powder

¼ tsp (1 mL) salt

1 cup (250 mL) blueberries

¾ cup (175 mL) cream-style corn

1 cup (250 mL) low-fat milk

¼ cup (50 mL) half-and-half
cream

1 egg, beaten

2 tbsp (25 mL) liquid honey

2 tbsp (25 mL) butter

Blend the cornmeal, flour, baking powder and salt in a big bowl. Spoon a couple of tablespoons of your flour mixture over the blueberries and stir lightly to coat them. This way they mingle better when they're introduced to the dry mixture. In another bowl collect the corn, milk and cream, and stir in the beaten egg. Melt the honey and butter together in the microwave and stir the mixture into the corn mess. Pour the wet stuff into the dry stuff and don't stir too much, just enough to moisten the dry stuff. Drop the batter into greased muffin cups and bake at 425°F (220°C) for 25 minutes—a little less if you left out the blueberries. Let cool in the pan 5 to 10 minutes, then cool on a rack. Makes 12–16 muffins, depending on the blueberries.

Muffins get tough if you stir too much.
Count 25 strokes and leave it at that.

*P*ity the poor egg. Even cooked, it's not as popular as it was. High-fat, high-cholesterol, eggs have had bad press. Recommended intake for just about anyone is four to six eggs a week, a far cry from the old egg diet—remember that?—which required you to eat *nine* eggs, and that was just the first day!

The question is now, in which basket are you going to put your eggs? Sunday brunch with Eggs Benedict? That's Fat City, but maybe you'd settle for my take-out version, with half an English muffin, no bacon or ham and a poached egg topped with a low-fat slice of cheese. Still troublesome, with 2 pans to wash.

Eggs really are quite nutritious, packing a lot of goodies into just 80 or 90 calories. One egg also gives you three-quarters of a day's supply of clogging cholesterol, but cheer up: the cholesterol is only in the *yolk*. You can substitute two egg whites for one whole egg and still get some protein.

Call this Eggs in a Cloud or

EGGS BENEDICTION

½ cup (125 mL) or so leftover fish or chicken (optional)

1 stalk celery, chopped

¼ green pepper, chopped

a wee drop of Worcestershire sauce

1 slice bread, toasted

2 egg whites, beaten until stiff

1 tbsp (15 mL) grated Parmesan cheese

Combine your leftovers with the celery and green pepper and a moistening of the Wooster. Pile onto the toast and top with the egg whites into which you have folded the cheese. Spread the egg white right to the edges of the toast, sealing in the filling. If you like, you can waft a little more cheese on top before you pop it into the toaster-oven set at 350°F (180°C) for 6 to 8 minutes to cook the meringue. If you decide against the leftovers but like the idea of the cloud on toast, put a surprise in the middle: salsa, hot or mild; imitation or real bacon bits; a few chopped mushrooms preheated in a little chicken stock, but drained, not wet. I like that one.

A WORD ABOUT EGGS: 2 egg whites can be substituted for 1 yolk. Add 1 tsp (5 mL) vegetable oil or 2 egg whites for each egg yolk omitted.

I did some experimenting with egg whites and here is a yolk-less omelet for you.[6]

EGG WHITE OMELET

3 egg whites

1 tbsp (15 mL) water

1 tbsp (15 mL) salad oil

1 tbsp (15 mL) green pepper, finely chopped

1 tbsp (15 mL) grated low-fat mozzarella cheese

freshly ground black pepper

Whip the egg whites, water and oil together and pour into an omelet pan spritzed with oil and pre-

6 *WHAT ABOUT ALL THOSE UNUSED EGG YOLKS? THEY'RE GOOD FOR A PET'S SHINY COAT, SO STIR SOME INTO THE PET FOOD. HERE'S ONE I JUST LEARNED FROM MARGIE KRESCHOLLEK: DILUTE EGG YOLKS WITH WATER AND USE THE MIXTURE AS PLANT FOOD. I JUST STARTED DOING IT, SO THE RETURNS AREN'T IN YET.*

heated on high heat. Mix the green pepper, cheese and black pepper together and wait a moment. Keep lifting the edges and tipping the egg to the sides of the pan just as you would for an ordinary omelet. Do that until the edges are beginning to dry but the centre is still moist. Sprinkle the filling over the eggs and keep lifting and tipping. As the egg whites set, start folding up one side towards the other. It should be cooked as you complete the fold. Lever gently onto a plate. It really works!

Here's a butterless egg, retaining the yolk:

BUTTERLESS EGG

> 1–2 tbsp (15–25 mL) water
>
> 1 egg
>
> 1 tbsp (15 mL) grated mozzarella cheese OR
>
> 1 tbsp (15 mL) snipped green onions OR
>
> 2 tbsp (25 mL) partially cooked sliced mushrooms

With a fork, whip the water into the egg in a microwave dish. Cook for 2 minutes on Medium in the microwave. Remove and add the cheese or the green onions or the mushrooms (which have been preheated with a melted chicken cube). Stir the mixture with a fork, bringing the cooked edges to the centre of the dish. Microwave for another minute and serve. Fat-free, but not cholesterol-free.

When I was doing my Old Lady Caper I sprouted my own alfalfa. Someone had given me a sprouter for a joke and on impulse I had taken it with me. I found space for it on top of the wardrobe in my tiny rented room and I started farming. Suddenly I had a forest of sprouts, almost for free. I concocted an egg dish with them that I remain devoted to.

SPROUTIE SPECIAL

1 tbsp (15 mL) or less butter (optional)

1 slice low-fat cheese OR

2 tbsp (25 mL) grated Cheddar cheese

1 egg

dash of Worcestershire sauce

a handful or more of alfalfa sprouts

I used to start this off with butter in a small cast-iron skillet. Now I spray the bottom swiftly and sparingly with oil, put in the cheese and turn on the heat. (You can use the butter if you don't care.) As the cheese begins to melt, drop in the egg and break the yolk immediately. Season with the Wooster and stir it with a wooden spoon as you drop in as many alfalfa sprouts as the mixture will uncomfortably hold.[7] It's a scrambled egg but it looks like an omelet because the sprouts form an armature to give it shape. Serve with a piece of toast. I really like this, but it takes all kinds of tastes to make a cookbook and I'll understand if you don't.

7 *I MEAN, UNCOMFORTABLY. THE POOR EGG IS STUFFED TO ITS EPIGLOTTIS WITH SPROUTS.*

On the whole, it's not a bad idea to stay away from fat for breakfast. That's why oatmeal porridge is such a good idea, especially if you mix your quick-cooking oats with oat bran. Rumour has it that oat bran actually lowers the cholesterol level, but it depends which nutritionist you read. Anyway, it's quick and easy in the microwave.

MICROATMEAL

¼ cup (50 mL) combined quick oats
and oat bran

½ cup (125 mL) water

pinch salt

about 1 tbsp (15 mL) raisins

maple syrup to taste

Combine the oats, water and salt in a serving bowl and zap for 2 minutes on Medium in the microwave. Stir in the raisins and enough maple syrup to moisten. Zap another minute and she's yours. You can skip the syrup and use milk and brown sugar if that suits you better. I know someone who uses soymilk.

Grits is (are?) a Southern dish that you cain't hardly get up north. You can substitute cornmeal, not quite as gritty or good for you, but low-fat at least, and delicious. You start by making cornmeal mush, or *polenta* (which is the Italian for cornmeal mush):

POLENTA

½ cup (125 mL) quick-cooking yellow
cornmeal

½ cup (125 mL) cold water

½ tsp (2 mL) or less salt

2 cups (500 mL) boiling water

Put the cornmeal in a saucepan and stir the cold water into it with the salt. Pour the boiling water over the cornmeal, stirring all the while to prevent lumps. Raise the heat until the mixture bubbles and then turn it to low. Cook 5 minutes, stirring frequently. You can either give yourself a serving of mush right now, with corn syrup or maple syrup, or pack it all into a small buttered loaf pan, cover and chill.

Use it for breakfast, lunch or supper, your choice. Cut a couple of slices and put it on a microwave dish with a generous sprinkle of grated Parmesan, Asiago or Cheddar cheese on top. Heat for no more than a minute. (The fat alternative is to fry the slices in butter, which I used to do before I knew better.) You can go sweet, sharp or salty with this. Instead of cheese try salsa—cold on the hot mush; or corn or maple syrup; or gravy.[8]

Polenta keeps well in the fridge for several days and there are other things you can do with it, like put other things on top of it.[9]

Chocolate bread pudding (p. 17) is another unorthodox breakfast, because it's usually classified as dessert, but think about it. It has bread and milk and eggs, which most traditional breakfasts comprise. If you can't stand chocolate that early in the morning, leave it out.[10] Here's a simpler, blander pudding, using up leftover breads.

BREAKFAST BREAD PUDDING

3–4 cups (750 mL–1 L) stale bread or buns, torn up into chunks

milk to moisten

4 eggs

8 YOU STILL EAT **GRAVY**?

9 IN MY OTHER LIFE I USED TO STIR A HALF POUND OF PORK SAUSAGE MEAT INTO THE CORNMEAL AS IT COOKED AND LATER SLICED AND FRIED IT FOR DINNER. IT'S CALLED **SCRAPPLE**.

10 I KNOW ONE PERSON WHO EATS LEFTOVER CHOCOLATE CAKE FOR BREAKFAST. NO, NOT ME! MY DAUGHTER KATE WOULD KILL ME IF I TOLD YOU WHO.

2 cups (500 mL) milk

1 tsp (5 mL) vanilla

½ cup (125 mL) brown sugar

a dollop of butter OR

1 tbsp (15 mL) vegetable oil

1 apple, peeled and chopped
(optional)

1 tsp (5 mL) cinnamon, if using the
apple

¼ cup (50 mL) apple syrup or light
maple syrup

In a large bowl, moisten the chunks of bread with a little milk—just pour over, stirring once—to soften the staleness. If you take a day or so to collect your bread, store the bowl, covered, in the fridge. When ready to cook it, dump the bread in a greased (or spritzed) 1½-quart casserole. Beat the eggs and 2 cups (500 mL) milk. Stir in the vanilla and brown sugar. Now you have a choice to make. You can bake it plain with the butter or oil on top to crisp the surface, giving it 35 minutes in a 350°F (180°C) oven. Or you can toss the apple in cinnamon and stir it into the mixture, pouring apple or maple syrup on top before baking. Obviously, this makes more than one serving. Store it in individual servings and freeze it if you like, but it's so good fresh, moist and warm, why not have some more for dessert tonight, and finish it off for tomorrow's breakfast? Warm it in the microwave each time, adding a little milk if it's dry. Any time, breakfast, dessert or snack, it's very comforting.

Speaking of comfort, do not forget hot cocoa. There are delicious hot chocolate mixes on the market now, including white chocolate. I have a friend who combines a chocolate mix with instant coffee for her own instant mocha starter. And don't forget café au lait. They make cups the size of chamber pots now for this imported fad, not an unhealthy one, providing as it does a good-sized serving of milk. Pour equal amounts of coffee and milk into a microwave-safe cup and heat the mixture until it's piping hot. Add, for fun, a dash of vanilla, or a sprinkle of cinnamon or grated chocolate, or stir it with a cinnamon stick.[11]

I cannot let breakfast go by without a word for cheese. A slice of low-fat cheese broiled on a piece of whole wheat toast is a very healthy, satisfying meal that takes care of the empty feeling without too many calories or fat grams. The continental breakfast in most European countries includes cheese. North Americans may not be ready for blood sausage, eel or herring, but cheese is always palatable. If you agree with that, then consider this: leftover cheese pizza. It may not be entirely regal but it's filling, fast and edible.

What remains in my memory of Cher in the movie *Mermaids* is her character's cooking: she made finger food. Everything looked like cocktail canapés or teatime tidbits, even breakfast. Not a bad idea. You may yet be able to do your hair (or shave) and eat at the same time (not that I approve).

Consider first what to use as the edible foundation of a good sturdy no-drip finger food, something to build on:

° English muffins, split and toasted

° bagels, split and toasted

11 *HAVEN'T YOU EVER RECEIVED A BOUQUET OF CINNAMON STICKS FOR CHRISTMAS WITH DIRECTIONS FOR MULLED WINE? DUST YOURS OFF AND USE ONE NOW.*

° individual pizza rounds

° pita bread, also called pockets

° Pillsbury crescent rolls, baked around something

° Pillsbury biscuit wraps, ditto

Now think about what you could put into or onto such carriers that could be considered breakfast food:

° grated cheese (low-fat)

° a thick slice of tomato

° lean cold cuts

° crisp bacon

° fried egg (think twice)

° peanut butter

° cream cheese (even light is heavy), topped with a slice of pineapple?

° chopped apple and cinnamon, and maybe a few raisins?

° jam

° chocolate chips or

° grated semi-sweet chocolate (for the croissants)[12]

Some of my interviews with random breakfasters yielded solutions you may or may not want to try, like the old hot-water-and-lemon trick.[13] Some people—all right, one—like leftovers for breakfast. I read years ago that writer-broadcaster Adrienne

12 OKAY, I WOULDN'T DO THIS, BECAUSE IT'S FAT AND FATTENING. BUT IT MIGHT BE GOOD IN BED.

13 FAILING THAT, AT LEAST DRINK AN ENTIRE GLASS OF WATER WITH YOUR VITAMINS.

Clarkson eats leftovers for her first meal, preferring Chinese food. I wouldn't mind some of my favourites in the morning but they're already gone. But here's what you can do with a few old pancakes:

PANCAKE SURPRISE

2 or 3 cooked pancakes (from the freezer?)

1 or 2 slices low-fat cheese OR

leftovers (Chinese?) OR

brown sugar and cinnamon with or without

1 apple, peeled and chopped

Lay a pancake in a small microwaveable dish. Place a slice of cheese on it, or spread it with plum or hoisin sauce and arrange some appealing leftovers on it, or mix the brown sugar and cinnamon and sprinkle that generously over it. Top with a second pancake (if you think you can eat more than that, repeat the layer and top with a third). Drop a dollop or less of butter on top to moisten it, or another cheese slice, or a dribble of soy sauce, or a little light maple syrup, choice of topping depending on choice of filling. Heat in the microwave on Medium-High about 1 minute. If the pancakes are very thin, you could sprinkle each one with brown sugar and roll it up like a cigar. Good hot or cold.

I have one last suggestion but brace yourself.

14 I AM INDEBTED TO DAVID ZIMMER
AT *COTTAGE LIFE* MAGAZINE FOR
ALLOWING ME TO USE THIS
RECIPE, WHICH HE SAYS DOES
NOT ORIGINATE WITH HIM BUT
WHICH HE HAS PASSED ON FOR
THE BENEFIT OF ALL COTTAGERS.
HE CALLS IT A LUMBERJACK
SPECIAL AND PRESCRIBES HEAVY
CLOSE-THE-COTTAGE WORK AND
LATE-SEPTEMBER RAINY WEATHER
AS JUSTIFICATION FOR THIS
"PROPER BREAKFAST AT THE
LAKE."

MONTE CRISTO SANDWICH[14]

2 eggs

2 tbsp (25 mL) flour

½ cup (125 mL) milk

salt and pepper

8 slices buttered bread

4 slices Black Forest ham

4 slices cheese (old Cheddar, Monterey Jack)

⅓ cup (75 mL) butter

lots of maple syrup

In a shallow dish, blend eggs, flour, milk, salt and pepper. On each of four slices of the bread arrange one slice each of ham and cheese. Cover with remaining bread slices to form a sandwich, and dip each one into the egg mixture, coating both sides thoroughly. Melt butter in a skillet and fry the sandwiches in it, browning them well on both sides. Serve at once drenched with maple syrup. You'll note this makes four sandwiches. Yes, you can make it for one but you won't feel as guilty if you share this rule-breaking, fast-breaking meal.

Everyone is entitled once in a while to breakfast like a portly monarch instead of a sensible king.

CHAPTER SEVEN

Lunch

For some reason, noboby seems to write much about lunch.

~ *Margaret Atwood*

Did I suggest that breakfast is the most idiosyncratic meal of the day? I was wrong. Lunch is. People tend to get very set in their habits about breakfast, but lunch is up for grabs, depending on the where-when-what-who parameters, plus how much money you have. Sufficient unto each day is the solution thereof, and that goes even more so for lunch. Lunch for singles may not appear to be the problem that breakfast or dinner is, that is, if you simply plan to go out and buy it. For the rest of you who have to prepare lunch—portable or otherwise—I say, make it something to look forward to.

Lunch is a good time for healthy things: soups in the winter;[1] salads in the summer; and of course the

1 *"OF SOUP AND LOVE," GOES THE SPANISH PROVERB, "THE FIRST IS BEST." IF SOUP IS TOO HOT, YOU ONLY BURN YOUR TONGUE. I LOVE HOT SOUP.*

ubiquitous sandwich, but let's see if we can come up with a filling other than peanut butter and banana, or North America's standby—tuna salad. Lunch is also good for leftovers, which, of course, brings us right back to soups, salads and sandwiches. Also finger foods. The main thing to remember about lunch is no one wants to wash a lot of dishes. If you can reduce your utensils to a spoon, that's a plus.

This book has many reminders to make soup stock, to spare the landfill and store vegetable parings and celery tops for stock, to get your money's worth and save the liquid drained from cans of vegetables. When do you get to eat all this lovely liquid vitamin elixir? Lunch is when. And it's a good thing because otherwise it would go sour on you. As long as you bring your soup to the boil every (or almost every) day, it will last a week or more in the fridge, so don't think you're saving electricity by heating only one mug for you.

Add things to it: deliberate, chopped things like more celery and carrots or broken-up sticks of pasta; almost planned things like the last of the rice you cooked this week or some leftover veggies—almost anything except beets (because of the colour), unless you add cabbage and turn it into borscht. Leftover cauliflower makes a statement all by itself, processed and poured into chicken stock, with or without curry.

If you are philosophically opposed to making your own soup stock, then check your can cupboard. A few of your basic soups make adequate lunches and become more interesting with the addition of something you probably have on hand. The basic rule for lunch is, don't go and buy anything just for lunch, unless you're having company.[2]

INTERESTING SOUPS FOR LUNCH

° Heat slightly thinned canned mushroom soup[3] with milk, heat until almost
  boiling, then slip an egg in to poach.

3 OR USE CREAM OF CHICKEN OR
CREAM OF CELERY.

° Toast a thick slice of French bread, put
  it in an individual oven-to-table dish,
  pour hot onion soup (from a can or
  mix) over it and a blizzard of grated
  Parmesan or Asiago, then broil until
  the cheese is stringy and oozy.

° Mix a minuscule can of chicken or
  turkey flakes in a can of undiluted
  cream of chicken soup and heat
  through in the microwave. Stir in some
  leftover peas or a little chopped celery.

° Same as above, but put it in an oven-
  proof dish, warm it first, and then top
  it with packaged pastry or biscuit
  dough and bake it like a chicken pie in
  the toaster-oven.

° Heat a can of minestrone with an
  obscene amount of basil or coriander
  pesto (p. 186).

° Thin a small can of cream-style corn
  with a little milk and heat for a simple
  soup.

LUNCH SALADS

Salads are good for leftovers, specifically the kind
with a rice or pasta base. You have cooked rice in
the fridge, so try this:

RICE SALAD

1 cup (250 mL) or less cooked rice

½ to 1 cup (125 to 250 mL) leftover vegetables

2 tbsp (25 mL) chopped Spanish onion OR 2 or 3 green onions, tops and bottoms, snipped

½ green pepper, chopped

2 stalks celery, chopped

¼ cup (50 mL) vinaigrette dressing (p. 87) OR 2 tbsp (25 mL) rice wine vinegar

1 tsp (5 mL) chopped fresh dill (optional)

You don't have to do much for this one: just inspect the fridge, chop a few things, toss and eat. It wouldn't be bad stuffed into a pita bread.

PASTA SALAD

1 cup (250 mL) or less cooked pasta

2 stalks celery, chopped

1/2 cup (125 mL) chopped green and red pepper

6–8 black olives, chopped (optional)

1 tbsp (15 mL) light mayo

1 tbsp (15 mL) low-fat yogurt

salt to taste

This is a basic recipe. You can add any leftover cooked vegetables that appeal to you: peas or corn niblets, asparagus cut in inch-lengths, green or wax beans. Mix the mayo and yogurt together and toss with the pasta and veggies. If your contents exceed the limits of the dressing, moisten it with a little rice wine vinegar. Both these salads ripen nicely, but when I get tired of something the same old way I add a piquant sauce, not necessarily Szechuan, or some grated cheese to the last of it and heat it in the microwave.

Here are a couple of more formal salads. I had to go to Greece to learn how to make a Greek salad properly. I'll save you the trip.

GREEK SALAD

> 4 or 5 romaine lettuce leaves, torn into bite-sized pieces
>
> 1 green pepper, cut into chunks
>
> 1 cucumber, peeled, cut into chunks
>
> 1 medium tomato(or 2 small) cut into chunks
>
> black olives
>
> freshly ground black pepper
>
> ½ cup (125 mL) feta cheese

The secret is in the proportion and size of the vegetables: not nearly as much lettuce as the rest of the ingredients and all about the same size—good-sized bites. I use some of the marinade from the olives for my dressing (see p. 70), so it's loaded with oregano, perhaps cut with a little lemon juice, perhaps with a little more oil added, but very little. The salad creates its own dressing. Perhaps this amount will serve a big appetite; I usually have a couple of meals' worth left over and eat it until it's gone, pouring off excess liquid if necessary. It's wonderful with warm garlic bread and a glass of red wine, nice for dinner too (have bread pudding for dessert that night).

Here's another cosmopolitan salad which I had to go to France to learn how to make. It's nice for lunch.

SALAD NIÇOISE

a couple of potatoes, peeled, cooked and diced large

1 serving of green beans, cooked until tender-crisp

1 hard cooked egg

1 can (4.7 oz/133 g) water-packed chunk tuna, drained

a bed of lettuce

vinaigrette dressing

If you're artistic, you can make this look terrific, putting the tuna chunks in the centre of the lettuce bed, strewing the potatoes and green beans in strategic places around it, decorating it with wedges of the egg, drizzling a small amount of the dressing over all. You will have some of this left over, but it keeps well for another lunch.

Here's a luncheon salad I developed one recent summer, and now I'm addicted:

RED FRUIT SALAD

3 or 4 radicchio leaves

1 or 2 Anjou pears, peeled and quartered

1 small red onion, thinly sliced

handful of raisins

apple cider vinegar fruit dressing

This is totally self-explanatory except the dressing. It began with a fancy bottle of fruit vinaigrette my niece gave me but after it was gone I made my own, blending ¼ cup (50 mL) apple cider vinegar with 2 tbsp (25 mL) of liquid honey.

Want a fast, fattening salad for company lunch?

AVOCADO INIQUITY FOR TWO

1 avocado

a smidge of lemon juice

½ cup (125 mL) low-fat sour cream

1 small jar (50 g) lumpfish caviar

alfalfa sprouts

cherry tomatoes

Halve the avocado, remove the stone and share the lemon juice between the two halves to keep them from going brown. Place each half on a plate, divide

4 MIGHT AS WELL GO FULL THROTTLE.

the sour cream between the two cavities and top with a dollop of caviar. Surround each half with artfully strewn alfalfa sprouts and a few cherry tomatoes and serve with warm croissants[4] and a glass of chilled white wine.

Now let's move on to slightly more sensible but just as tempting solutions to the lunch question. With my penchant for putting things into or onto things, I suggest filling your hollow by filling other appealing hollows—and so we come back to finger foods.

Cold or hot, finger foods ooze across the lines of etiquette.[5] Consider what you can put in or on things to heat for a movable no-dish feast for one.

5 I HAVE READ THAT THE REAL TEST OF A PERSON'S REFINEMENT IS THE WAY HE OR SHE EATS WHEN ALONE: SITTING PROPERLY, USING A NAPKIN AND THE PROPER UTENSILS, NEVER PUTTING A CARTON OR A JAR ON THE TABLE AND NEVER, EVER DRINKING OUT OF A CARTON OR PITCHER (MY HUSBAND USED TO DO THIS). NONE OF THESE RULES APPLIES TO A SINGLE PERSON EATING LUNCH.

Potentially hot:

- ° individual pizza rounds
- ° pita bread, aka pockets (whole wheat, please)
- ° tart shells
- ° tortillas
- ° a cooked potato skin
- ° a biscuit wrap
- ° rice cakes

Cold is good, too:

- ° a large whole tomato, scooped out
- ° a hard-cooked egg, halved, yolk removed
- ° half a cantaloupe, seeds removed

Your assignment, should you choose to accept it, is to fill one or more of these containers. Most of these are excellent vehicles for leftovers, too. Feel free to embellish, add, jazz up and improvise. Just don't make it too drippy.

Here are some suggestions and recipes.

Pizza

Spread salsa or tomato sauce on the pizza and build from there with chopped:

- ° tomatoes

- ° green pepper

- ° mushrooms

- ° anchovies[6]

- ° pepperoni slices

- ° sliced luncheon meat

And finally, grated:

- ° mozzarella

- ° Parmesan

6 *THERE MAY BE SOME IN THE FREEZER TO USE UP.*

Tuna Salad for Pizza Rounds

- ° 1 (4.7 oz/133 g) can water-packed tuna, drained

- ° 1 clove garlic, crushed

- ° ½ cup (125 mL) chopped fennel bulb (optional)

- ° 1 tbsp (15 mL) lemon juice

- ° 1 tbsp (15 mL) olive oil

Pita Pockets

Stuff with Feta-Garlic Crumbles (p. 96) and leftover cooked spinach and heat in the microwave.

Also good in the pocket are sliced:
- ° avocado
- ° tomatoes
- ° cheese
- ° alfalfa sprouts

Tuna Filling for Pita Bread

This makes enough for two or three lunches. Take a pita to work and zap it there.[7]

1 can (4.7 oz/133 g) water-packed tuna, drained

2 stalks celery, finely chopped

1 tbsp (15 mL) light mayo, mixed with

1 tbsp (15 mL) low-fat yogurt

½ tsp (2 mL) sage

Curried Eggs for Pita Pockets[8]

2 hard-cooked eggs, sliced, gently stirred into:

1 can (10 oz/284 mL) cream of chicken soup, seasoned with 1 tsp (5 mL) curry powder

3 or 4 sliced mushrooms (optional)

7 TRUST ME, WARM TUNA SALAD IN A PITA POCKET IS DELICIOUS. YOU COULD EVEN ADD A COUPLE TBSP OF GRATED CHEESE TO MELT IN WITH IT.

8 YES, YES, YOU'RE GOING TO SAY THIS IS TOO MUCH FOR ONE PITA POCKET. DON'T YOU NEED SOMEONE TO CHANGE AN UNREACHABLE LIGHT BULB (IF YOU'RE FEMALE) OR DARN A SOCK (IF YOU'RE MALE)?—NO, NO, THAT'S SEXIST. LET'S SEE: SCREW THE TEMPLE BAR ON YOUR GLASSES BECAUSE YOU DON'T HAVE THAT SMALL A SCREWDRIVER; LOOK UP SOMETHING FOR YOU IN A

Curried Lentils for Pita Pockets

½ cup (125 mL) cooked lentils, mixed with

1 tbsp (15 mL) oil, heated to release the flavour of

2 green onions, snipped, and

1 tsp (5 mL) curry powder, plus

½ cup (125 mL) chopped apple (optional)

DICTIONARY YOU DON'T OWN; HELP YOU MOVE YOUR BED SO YOU CAN PAINT THE WALL BEHIND IT; BE ON THE OTHER SIDE OF THE NET FOR A TENNIS GAME? THE POINT IS, HAVE SOME CASUAL COMPANY AND FEED HIM/HER. OR FACE THIS FACT, AS I HAVE POINTED OUT: ENJOY IT WHILE IT'S WITH YOU, WHICH MAY BE SEVERAL DAYS.

TART SHELLS

Mushroom Tart Filling

½ cup (125 mL) chopped mushrooms

½ tsp (2 mL) dried dill or tarragon

¼ cup (50 mL) low-fat yogurt

Ham Tart Filling

½ cup (125 mL) chopped canned ham or luncheon meat

2 green onions, snipped

1 tbsp (15 mL) brown sugar, mixed with ½ tsp (2 mL) dry mustard OR 2 tbsp (25 mL) grated Cheddar cheese mixed with 1 tsp (5 mL) wet mustard

Mound the above fillings into baked tart shells and zap them in the microwave just to warm up the innards.

The following fillings have to be baked on account of the Egg Beaters. Bake them at 375°F (190°C) for about 20 minutes—surprisingly long, considering their size, but true. Rather than mixing the ingredients into the egg mixture, just sprinkle them in the tart shells and pour the egg over them. If your shells are very small, you'll find the amount suggested will fill about four shells.

Chicken or Turkey Tart Filling

½ cup (125 mL) chopped cooked chicken or turkey

1 stalk celery, chopped

1 green onion, snipped

¼ cup (50 mL) Egg Beaters, fork-whipped

½ tsp (2 mL) Worcestershire sauce

Tuna Tart Filling

½ cup (125 mL) chopped drained water-packed chunk tuna

2 or 3 mushrooms, chopped

1 tbsp (15 mL) soy sauce

¼ cup (50 mL) Egg Beaters, fork-whipped

Quiche Tart Filling

½ cup (125 mL) Egg Beaters, fork-whipped

2 tsp (10 mL) real bacon bits (optional)

¼ cup (50 mL) grated mozzarella
cheese

2 green onions, snipped

TORTILLAS

° Layer a soft tortilla with low-fat sour
cream, sliced smoked salmon, a squirt
of lemon juice and a sprinkling of
chopped fresh dill.[9]

° You can also heat a tortilla with something tucked and rolled into it, such as:
    chopped leftover chicken or turkey
    chopped green pepper
    chopped tomato
    chopped avocado
    salsa
    refried beans
    grated cheese

9 *AREN'T YOU GLAD YOU DON'T
HAVE TO SHARE?*

POTATO SKINS

Use leftover baked potatoes (see p. 206), saving a fair
bit of flesh on the skin. Spread with any of the following and heat in the microwave:

° salsa

° nacho cheese spread OR grated
mozzarella

° low-fat sour cream and bacon bits

° a few chopped mushrooms, tossed with
grated Parmesan

BISCUIT WRAP

Things to stick in a biscuit wrap:

- ° wiener (?)
- ° cheese
- ° chopped raisins or dates

RICE CAKES

A new fad among low-fat noshers. One young woman I interviewed cited a rice cake as the basis for lunch or supper, simply:

- ° 1 rice cake spread with drained canned tuna, topped with 1 slice cheese, and melted[10]

10 YOU HAVE TO EAT THIS WITH YOUR FINGERS AND TEETH. YOU CAN'T CUT A RICE CAKE WITH A KNIFE AND FORK. CATCH THE DRIP WITH A NAPKIN.

11 DROP THE PULP IN YOUR SALSA OR SPAGHETTI SAUCE.

TOMATO SHELLS

Scoop out a large tomato[11] and fill with what appeals to you:

- ° low-fat cottage cheese with snipped chives or green onions
- ° canned salmon, mashed up, bones and all OR drained canned water-packed tuna
- ° leftover rice salad

HARD-COOKED EGG

Halve the egg, scoop out the yolk and fill the hollows with the rest of the caviar from that iniquitous lunch (see avocado p. 129) Sprinkle a little of the crumbled egg yolk on top. Or try raw chopped mushrooms with tarragon.

CANTALOUPE

Halve the melon and remove the seeds. Fill one half with cottage cheese or—super-indulgence!—with vanilla ice cream. Or fill with a combination of any fruit in season, cut up. Or mound in the last of your chicken salad.

Of course, the ultimate finger food is a sandwich, but I hesitate to mention it because it is so obvious. Very few sandwiches are intended to be eaten with knife and fork. Hot meat sandwiches with gravy, Reubens with oozing sauerkraut and cheese, obscenely big hamburgers hanging over the sides of a poor little (cowed?) bun—all these require surgery. I prefer to think about delectable fillings designed to go between two slices or on top of one piece of delicious, interesting bread.

Canned tuna and salmon and peanut butter are among the most popular sandwich fillings. Few people mention sardines, although the calcium count is great. I personally think sardines teeter on the edge of infinity. One tin of sardines for one consumer is about three times too much. Sardines on toast sounds like a very thirties lunch to me, and there's no disguising them. The sad thing about sandwiches is that all of you past a certain age—and even younger than that—have eaten thousands of them, and you're bored. The good thing is that they are easy to prepare, create almost no mess, use up stuff and contain a good variety of the food groups. Also, they go with milk and you have to drink at least one glass a day.

In my version of the ultimate finger food, I used to make watercress sandwiches and I actually ironed the bread for them! So I felt a tenuous kinship when I saw the movie *Bennie & Joon*, in which the Johnnie Depp character ironed his grilled cheese sandwiches. Sensible thing to do. Watercress butter is delicious and almost as easy to make as a cheese slice.

WATERCRESS BUTTER

> about 1 cup (250 mL) fresh watercress
>
> ¼ lb (125 g) cold butter
>
> salt to taste

Wash and drain the watercress, removing coarse stems. Stuff it into the processor bowl with the hard butter (cut into small pieces) and enough salt. Whirl it and pack it down, whirl it and pack it until you have a lovely homogeneous swirl of green butter.

Before you assemble the sandwiches be sure the watercress butter is soft enough that it won't rip the bread. Buy an unsliced loaf and slice it lengthwise, and remove the crusts. Iron the bread between sheets of waxed paper.[12] Butter each lengthwise slice liberally with the butter and roll up each slice as tightly as you can to make a jelly-roll-like package. Wrap each package in waxed paper and a tea towel and chill until ready to serve. Slice the rolls into

12 OR YOU CAN USE A ROLLING PIN OR A WINE BOTTLE.

little wheels. This is finger food for a time when you're feeling frivolous.[13]

13 *I KNOW THIS IS WORK-INTENSIVE BUT INDULGE ME.*

Dill butter is of course the same, only with fresh dill weed. Either of these butters is nice to have in the fridge in the summer, for sudden sandwiches, for garnishing a piece of fish, melting a tablespoon for taste into hot chicken soup, or even tossing a generous dollop with a bowl of pasta. They break every rule I ever made about butter and they're worth every fat gram!

I flipped through some old church cookbooks, the earnest collections of home recipes that church-women published to raise money for the Flower Fund or the Stained Glass Endowment, to get some new-old ideas about more robust sandwiches. Here's a list of suggestions for sandwich fillings to suit an older generation and awe a younger one.

SANDWICH FILLINGS

- chopped chicken, minced crisp bacon, mayo
- sliced chicken, tomatoes, mayo
- sliced chicken and lettuce
- sliced beef or lamb with chopped mustard pickle
- sliced meat loaf, chili sauce, lettuce
- chopped ham, minced pickles, mayo
- devilled ham (from a tin), pickle relish, mayo
- salmon, hard-cooked egg, mayo

° sardines mashed with lemon juice and minced green pepper

° peanut butter, chopped ginger, mayo

° grated carrots, peanut butter, mayo

° chopped raisins, figs and dates mixed with honey

° sliced tomatoes, lettuce, mayo (black pepper, please!)

° sliced cucumbers, thinly sliced onions, mayo

° creamed butter and brown sugar with cinnamon (toasted)

° peanut butter, honey and cream cheese (no mention of bananas with peanut butter)

Here are a few warm ones:

° Spread sliced bread with undiluted cream of mushroom soup, roll it and nail each sandwich shut with a toothpick before toasting in the toaster-oven[14]

° Roll canned asparagus spears in buttered bread slices, crusts removed, and broil until toasted

° Lay heated asparagus spears across a slice of toast, cover with a couple of slices of cheese and broil[15]

14 MY HUSBAND'S AUNT NELL USED TO MAKE THINGS LIKE THIS FOR US WHEN WE VISITED HER FOR LUNCH. I NEVER SAW IT IN A COOKBOOK.

15 ONE OF MY FAVOURITE LUNCHES, WITH LOW-FAT CHEESE.

Just because they've been with us for a long time doesn't mean that sandwiches don't still deserve a nod and a nosh. Do as the restaurants do: serve half a sandwich[16] with a cup of soup or a small salad (or crudités). Go back to work.

You can do a little real cooking for a delectable lunch. Only the first time will cost you any time and effort. I'm talking about quiche, if you can spare the eggs. Although I prefer a frittata these days, I still make quiche, and it's a very nourishing lunch. Left-over portions can be packaged individually and kept in the freezer not more than a month. They reheat beautifully in the microwave, staying moist. So here's a classic quiche, starting with a packaged frozen pastry shell.

CLASSIC QUICHE

1 partially baked 9-inch (23 cm) pie shell

10 strips bacon[17]

4 eggs

2 cups (500 mL) whipping cream or half-and-half

½ tsp (2 mL) salt

several grinds of black pepper

¼ tsp (1 mL) freshly grated nutmeg

2 cups (500 mL) grated Emmenthal cheese

17 OR YOU COULD SKIP THE BACON AND REPLACE IT WITH SPEARS OF COOKED ASPARAGUS.

Preheat the oven to 375°F (190°C). Fry the bacon[18] until partially cooked. Lay the strips in the pie shell. Beat the eggs, stir in the cream and seasonings, then add the cheese. Pour this thick mixture over the

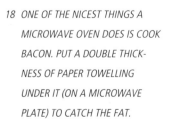

18 ONE OF THE NICEST THINGS A MICROWAVE OVEN DOES IS COOK BACON. PUT A DOUBLE THICK-NESS OF PAPER TOWELLING UNDER IT (ON A MICROWAVE PLATE) TO CATCH THE FAT.

bacon. Bake for 45 minutes. Makes 4 to 6 servings, to be frozen and savoured one slice at a time. To test for doneness, slip a knife into the centre. It should come out clean.

> **AN OUNCE OF PREVENTION**
> *Put a pan or a foil tray under your quiche pan in case of overflow and spare yourself hours on your knees in front of the oven.*

If you're in a quiche mood and don't want to go to all that bother, try a couple of tart shell quiches (p. 134). Incidentally, they make lovely, rich hors d'oeuvres to serve unexpected guests with a drink before a (simple) dinner.

I've mentioned frittata a number of times, making promises I haven't kept. Lunch is a good time for frittata. It's nice for brunch too, but singles don't have brunch as often as they have lunch. A frittata is Italian for omelet. It's a one-dish meal — cooked in a cast-iron skillet which can travel from stovetop to oven — and though it takes longer than five minutes to cook, it takes less than five to prepare.

BASIC FRITTATA

Choice of the following groups of ingredients:

- ° 1 small onion, sliced
- ° 2 cloves garlic, crushed
- ° 1 zucchini, sliced
- ° 1 green pepper, cut up
- ° 5 or 6 mushrooms, sliced
- ° several grinds of black pepper

OR

° cooked potatoes, diced

° green onions, snipped

° mushrooms

° ½ tsp (2 mL) tarragon

OR

° canned artichoke hearts, drained and
halved

° onion

° mushrooms

° a sloosh of salsa

Pre-heat the oven to 375°F (190°C). In a cast-iron skillet, melt a frozen chicken soup cube (or lightly spritz with salad oil). Start the onion and garlic first just to let them know who's in charge, then add other vegetables and let them get acquainted but not too soft-hearted, for no more than 5 minutes, stirring definitively.

Now for the eggs:

1 carton Egg Beaters, well shook up,
OR 4 eggs, fork-whipped

½ cup (125 mL) grated mozzarella
cheese

Stir half the cheese into the egg mixture and pour it all over the vegetables in the pan. Stir to mix everything, top the mixture with the rest of the cheese, and then slip the pan into the oven. Bake for about 25 minutes or until the eggs are set but not concrete.

Cut the frittata in quarters and eat it fresh the first time.

Leftovers:

> Freeze the other three quarters in three microwave dishes, covered with plastic wrap and foil. Lunch is even faster the next time round: straight from the freezer, remove the foil and vent the plastic, then give it 4 minutes in the microwave, top with a little extra grated cheese or salsa and warm that for a minute.

> *A TIP FROM JOHN WYLIE*
>
> *Sprinkle the bottom of a pie pan with a thick layer of dry bread crumbs. Pour a hot frittata mixture directly from its skillet over the crumbs before you bake it. It seasons the crumbs, and the liquid drains into them to form a delicious crust as it bakes. (My son is a great cook!)*

You may have perceived that anything goes with a frittata. Almost any combination of food, leftover or from scratch, rallied by an onion and garlic, can find its way into this comforting lunch.

Working or not, there are times when even the youngest among you might be feeling poorly and need not only comfort food, but also something bland, soft and good-tasting—in short, nourishing food that just lies there and doesn't challenge you.

I knew a very rich man who took a party to one of the most exclusive restaurants in New York one night when he wasn't feeling very well. He encouraged his guests to choose what they wanted but he asked the waiter if the chef could make milk toast for him. The chef produced the most exquisite milk toast I have ever seen, and served it elegantly. (I'm sure it had an elegant price tag, too.) The point is, that into every life, whatever the cost, a little milk toast must fall.

MILK TOAST

2 thick slices good bread

a dollop of butter

salt OR cinnamon OR nutmeg mixed with sugar

1 cup (250 mL) hot milk

Toast the bread lightly, spread with butter and sprinkle with the salt or sugar mixture. Lay the toast side by side in a shallow dish and pour hot milk over it.

There are other simple lunches that don't even occur to people who are accustomed to everything in packages or cans. A survey, this time among people who grew up during the Depression, has turned up some amazing ideas for lunch, cheap, not terribly nutritious if you don't add a piece of fruit or a vitamin, but filling, easy, edible and with no leftovers. Bet you never thought of serving rice pudding for lunch, with or without raisins; or bread and milk (cubes of bread sprinkled with sugar with milk poured over); oats soaked overnight in milk with a cut-up apple or other fruit (a simplified muesli); or French toast (everyone thinks it's for breakfast). Plain egg noodles, boiled and tossed with butter and salt, also served as lunch in simpler times. They're comforting too.

Now go from cheap, bland comfort to the other extreme. Antipasti make a gorgeous lunch, but not too often because it's expensive food and loaded with fat. But for a good nosh, plan lunch with a beer in front of a sportscast or a favourite movie and eat your fill from a tray loaded with any or all of the following:

- ° cold cuts: salami, summer sausage, mortadella

- ° tuna, straight out of the can, merely drained

- ° olives

- ° dill pickles

- ° sliced tomatoes

- ° cheeses: Brie, Gorgonzola, blue, Stilton, Oka, Cheddar

- ° Dijon mustard/butter

- ° some great crusty bread

- ° grapes or an apple

Living alone, you have to go easy on the amounts and variety because the food will dry up before you can use it all. Good as it is, you'll get tired of it. If you take lunch to work, you could brown bag some of this stuff, but only if there's a refrigerator at your workplace, because it's pretty potent. You could also use it up during the week by eating it as hors d'oeuvres, but then you'd have to eat a pretty light dinner to follow, maybe a Wylie Waldorf salad (p. 76), thus finishing off that blue cheese while you're at it. (Getting good at that lateral thinking?)

Still in the Italian mode, why don't we all have a couple of slices of bruschetta?

BRUSCHETTA

a lengthwise slice of focaccia or French bread

olive oil

plum tomatoes, seeded and chopped

fresh basil, minced

4 cloves garlic, crushed

freshly ground black pepper

Dribble or—to use less—spritz the bread with olive oil. Mix the tomatoes, basil and garlic together, season to taste, and spread this on the bread.[19] Broil until bubbly. Cut into shorter lengths to serve. It's hard to stop at one.

I have several friends who solve the problem of lunch by fasting. I can't/won't do that for at least two reasons.

1) I need the break from the computer, to get up, go into another room, prepare something, eat it, and think about something else.

2) How would I ever get rid of my leftovers?

19 YOU COULD ALSO ADD A FEW OF YOUR LEFTOVER ANTIPASTI: OLIVES? CUT-UP MORTADELLA? CHEESE?

CHAPTER EIGHT

Dinner

Dinner is one of life's pleasures.

~ Laurie Colwin

This is where delicious decadence begins. This is what couples envy most when they tell you they envy you.[1] End of the day, home to your castle, shut away the world, kick off your shoes, sigh, and ask yourself, "What's for dinner?" The choice is yours.

Of course, anyone can broil a steak. But steak is an expensive, ultimately boring way to go, ditto lamb chops (28 grams of fat per chop, if you don't trim the fat off), veal chops, pork chops, cutlets, etc. Even the smallest piece of liver, calves' or beef, daunts a single.[2] If you still are a red-meat eater, you have to think fast, as in fast food, as in ground beef. To come in under the 15-minute time limit, you have to forget stewing beef and all the cheaper but slower cuts. Unless you have a crock pot. Unfortu-

1 AND THEY DO.

2 CHICKEN LIVERS ARE MORE
  FUN AND GIVE YOU MORE
  LEFTOVER OPTIONS.

nately, crock pots know no moderation. Mae West said you can never get too much of a good thing, but she wasn't talking about beef stew. Neither am I.

What I'm doing is offering you 60 simple entrées, fit for a single, often expandable to accommodate visiting children, a buddy or a lover, and possible to serve again another day if there's too much. I try to keep them simple, small and short term, that is, one-shot, but in those cases of a plethora, I offer leftover advice.

This is *serious*. This is *dinner*. Don't be discouraged. You need balance, persistence and consistent adherence to common-sense food rules.

But what if you feel like pigging out? If you can just head off temptation at the pass, that is, in the grocery store, refusing to buy Häagen-Dazs and croissants, skipping the Oreos and chips, thus saving a lot of money as well, then you'll be safe at home with temptation out of hips' way. Ask yourself this question when you're contemplating eating something you shouldn't: "Do I want to wear this for the next year?"

There are ways to dodge temptation, which rises most frequently before, during and after dinner. Here are a few snack ideas to help keep temptation and hunger at bay.

SENSIBLE SINGLE SNACKS

Spritzers: white wine with soda water or—fewer calories—orange or apple juice with soda water

Soup: a bowl of clear broth before a meal fills empty corners and fools you into eating less

Bloody Shames: a wonderfully spicy tomato or clamato juice without the vodka, garnished with a large celery stick to be eaten virtuously

Celery: speaking of which, stuff a stalk with seasoned cottage cheese, cut it into short lengths and eat it all up

Crudités: a tempting bowl full of lovely raw veggies—cauliflowerets and broccoli, cherry tomatoes, red and green pepper sticks, cucumber sticks or coins—keeps you munching and happy

Dip, if you must, the above, in something, but keep it simple, like low-fat yogurt seasoned with curry or garlic or dill

Strawberries: low-calorie treat, a favourite. Forget strawberry shortcake, but you could break down and dip one or two in a little melted chocolate. A few chocolate chips melted in the micro-wave aren't going to kill anyone

Popcorn: no butter

And don't forget

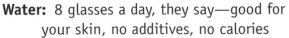

Water: 8 glasses a day, they say—good for your skin, no additives, no calories

PART ONE

Thirty Dinners for Carnivores

I have no doubt that it is part of the destiny of the human race, in its gradual improvement, to leave off eating animals, as surely as the savage tribes have left off eating each other when they came in contact with the more civilized.

~ *Henry David Thoreau*

I interviewed one single woman, divorced, children grown, back at school to upgrade her skills, who told me that if she didn't plan ahead, she wouldn't eat. She was too tired at the end of each day to think, let alone cook. She buys large economy packages of chicken breasts, for example, and on Sundays she poaches or broils them all, then slices, dices, arranges, packages and freezes the meat for a succession of meals, to be produced with almost no effort when the time comes.

I approved of her game plan and took it from there. Herewith my suggestions for Helga's chicken bounty.[3]

3 REMOVE THE SKIN FROM CHICKEN BEFORE YOU COOK IT, TO MINIMIZE THE FAT.

CHICKEN DIVAN

½ cup (125 mL) cooked brown rice[4]

1 serving of lightly cooked broccoli

1 cooked chicken breast, sliced

grated Parmesan cheese

4 THIS IS FOR A WEEK WHEN YOU HAVE BOILED AHEAD AND HAVE 2 CUPS (500 ML) COOKED RICE IN THE FRIDGE.

Remember I told you to cook the whole bunch of broccoli the first time round and then use the other serving(s) for other meals? This is one of those meals. Layer the rice in a microwave dish, spread the broccoli over it and arrange the chicken over that.[5] Cover with plastic wrap, vented,

> **STOP HERE!**
> At this point you can freeze the dinner. Of course, it will take a few minutes longer in the microwave then.

and heat in the microwave on High 3 minutes. Uncover, sprinkle with Parmesan cheese and zap again to melt the cheese.

5 BEFORE I LOWERED MY FAT GRAM COUNT I USED TO POUR BÉCHAMEL SAUCE ALL OVER THIS BEFORE I SPRINKLED IT WITH PARMESAN CHEESE. NOW I DON'T, BUT IF NECESSARY, YOU CAN DRIBBLE A LITTLE CHICKEN STOCK OVER IT TO MOISTEN THE RICE BEFORE YOU APPLY THE CHEESE.

Leftover Advice:

If you can't eat a whole chicken breast, either use less when you assemble the dish or make a sandwich for your brown bag the next day.

CHICKEN AND PASTA

1 serving of linguine or fusilli

a spritz of oil OR 1 frozen chicken soup cube OR 2 tbsp (25 mL) chicken broth

1 small onion, coarsely chopped

1 clove garlic, crushed

1 red pepper, cut in strips

1 cooked chicken breast, cut in strips

grated Parmesan or Romano cheese

Cook the linguine—for about 10 minutes—while you prepare the stir-fry. In a cast-iron skillet or a wok, heat the oil or stock, add the onion and garlic, soften them swiftly over medium heat and add the peppers, but don't let the peppers get soft. Raise the heat and add the chicken, stirring to heat through. Drain the pasta and toss it with the chicken mixture, topping with grated cheese to taste.

The 10-minute cook, Edouard de Pomiane, says you should put a pot of water on to boil the minute you walk in the door. Nights when you plan to have pasta, do that. Then the water will be ready to cook the linguine while you cut the chicken and red pepper. That is, if you want to eat so soon after you get home.

Leftover Advice:

If you made more than you can eat, store it in a microwave dish and reheat for lunch the next day. I usually add a little more cheese then, or a dash of something zippy.

CHICKEN CLUBHOUSE

This was my husband's recipe for a sandwich so big it deserves to be called dinner. Build it going up as the column reads down.

1 slice toast, buttered and spread with:

horseradish (optional)

sliced cooked chicken breast

dill pickles, thinly sliced

crisp bacon (optional)

1 slice toast, buttered both sides, upper side spread with mustard

Cheddar cheese, thinly sliced

tomato, thinly sliced

salt and freshly ground black pepper

lettuce

butter and mayonnaise spread on

1 slice toast

Cut in halves or quarters and anchor each section with a toothpick speared through a stuffed olive (optional). This meal is safer to eat at the table, because it drips.

Leftover Advice:
No advice. This *is* leftovers!

CHICKEN POT PIE

1 cooked chicken breast, cut into chunks

1 serving of frozen peas or mixed veg[6]

1 can (10 oz/284 mL) sliced mushrooms, drained OR 4 or 5 fresh mushrooms, thinly sliced

6 I NEVER PRECOOK A FROZEN VEGETABLE; WHATEVER COOKING IT GETS AS IT MEETS ITS DINNER PARTNERS DOES IT JUST FINE.

1 can (10 oz/284 mL) cream of chicken soup, diluted with 2 tbsp (25 mL) white wine or sherry (optional)

1 serving of biscuit dough (see package directions)

If there's just you, omit one of the veg; if you have company, add more. Combine everything but the biscuit dough in a small casserole.

STOP HERE!

Prepare this far the night before and refrigerate. Next day, continue with the topping when the mixture is warm.

Warm the contents (swiftly, on Low in the microwave), then top with the dough and bake in a preheated toaster-oven at 425°F (220°C) for 10 minutes, but watch it. The baking time might exceed our time limit, but it's worth it.

Leftover Advice:
Oh, for goodness' sake, eat it!

ORANGE CHICKEN STRIPS

1 clove garlic, crushed

½ tsp (2 mL) grated fresh ginger

2 tbsp (25 mL) frozen orange juice concentrate

1 cooked chicken breast, cut into strips

1 serving of frozen stir-fry vegetable mix

couple of frozen chicken soup cubes, as
required

cooked cellophane noodles[7]

In a microwave dish, zap the garlic and ginger in the
orange juice and then stir in the chicken, veg and
chicken cubes. Microwave the mixture on Medium
3 to 4 minutes, rotating and stirring once. Serve over
noodles.

CHICKEN TANDOORI

You can also cook chicken from scratch in an imitation Tandoori style, letting it stand in the paste for 1
hour, refrigerated, before broiling and basting
(20–30 minutes, turning every 10) but this Speed-
Scratch way tastes good and it's a lot faster.

1 cooked chicken breast

1 tbsp (15 mL) or more curry powder
(or make your own—see below)

½–⅓ cup (125–175 mL) light yogurt

8 *YOU USUALLY HAVE ONLY TWO
CHOICES FOR DISTANCE IN A
TOASTER-OVEN. CHOOSE THE
MORE DISTANT.*

Place the chicken on your toaster-oven broiling
pan. Whip the curry into the yogurt and spread it
thickly on the chicken. Broil it a fair distance from
the heat[8] turning once until the yogurt bubbles and
thickens, (about 3–4 minutes per side). Serve with
some of your cooked rice, warmed in chicken broth
to moisten, and with however many condiments
you have time or taste for, such as sliced tomatoes
and bananas with lime, chopped peanuts, mango
chutney, sliced kiwi.

A SIMPLE SAMPLE CURRY POWDER

It's easy to make your own curry seasoning, as hot and varied as you like. Hot oil or butter or a thawed frozen chicken soup cube will release the flavour to spike anything you care to cook: fish, lamb, beef, chicken, eggs, vegetables, whatever. Even a dish of thinly sliced onions tastes wonderful heated in a good curry paste. The seasoning may have as few as five spices or upwards of 25—herbs, seeds and spices. Here's a recent curry of mine, but don't feel curtailed.

> 1 tbsp (15 mL) turmeric
>
> 1 tbsp (15 mL) garlic powder
>
> 1 tsp (5 mL) salt
>
> 1 tsp (5 mL) whole cumin seed
>
> 1 tsp (5 mL) ground black pepper
>
> ½ tsp (2 mL) ground coriander
>
> ¼ tsp (1 mL) each ginger, cinnamon and allspice

You don't need a mortar and pestle; just whirl it up in your mini-processor. It will blend even more when it hits the hot soup or oil.

CHICKEN WITH SWEET POTATO

> 1 cooked sweet potato, sliced lengthwise
>
> 1 or 2 slices canned pineapple[9]
>
> 1 cooked chicken breast, sliced
>
> 2 rings green pepper
>
> pineapple juice or chicken broth, to moisten

9 IF YOU DON'T WANT TO OPEN A CAN OF PINEAPPLE AND/OR DON'T HAVE A GREEN PEPPER, THEN SPRINKLE SUNFLOWER SEEDS OVER THE SWEET POTATO AND USE A SPARING DASH OF BALSAMIC VINEGAR INSTEAD OF THE PINEAPPLE JUICE.

Spread a layer of sweet potato slices in a microwave dish and pour a little pineapple juice from the can on top to moisten. Zap on High for 2 minutes; remove and top the potato with pineapple. Layer slices of chicken over that, garnish with the green pepper. Moisten with juice or broth and zap again at Medium heat for 2 minutes until piping hot.

Leftover Advice:

> Use up the pineapple with cottage cheese for lunch, or cut it up and toss it with grated carrots moistened with the pineapple juice.

CHICKEN SZECHUAN PASTA

Remember to get your water boiling first while you do your chopping.

> 1 serving of fusilli
>
> 1 or 2 frozen chicken soup cubes OR a spritz of oil
>
> 2 or 3 stalks celery, cut up
>
> 1 or 2 green onions, snipped
>
> ½ green pepper, cut into chunks
>
> ½ cup (125 mL) fresh snow peas
>
> 1 cooked chicken breast, cut into chunks
>
> a sloosh of Szechuan sauce[10]

Cook the fusilli in boiling water (about 10 minutes). Meanwhile, heat the chicken stock or oil in a cast-iron skillet or a wok. Cook the vegetables first,

10 *DID YOU NOTICE I MANAGED TO WAIT UNTIL RECIPE NUMBER NINE BEFORE SPLASHING IN THE SZECHUAN SAUCE? I USE A WELL-KNOWN COMMERCIAL BRAND, BUT I CAN, IF NECESSARY, MAKE MY OWN AND YOU CAN TOO (SEE P. 75).*

on medium-high heat adding one group at a time, beginning with the onions, but with scarcely a pause, stir in the chicken to heat it up. Blend in the sauce last, and when everything is hot, toss it with the drained fusilli.

Leftover Advice:

> Leftovers are easy, reheated for lunch.

CHICKEN FRIED RICE

1 tbsp (15 mL) oil

1 egg

2 tsp (10 mL) soy sauce

2 or 3 stalks celery, cut up fine

2 or 3 green onions, snipped

1 cooked chicken breast, cut into smallish dice

½–1 cup (125–250 mL) cooked rice[11]

chicken stock to taste

11 DON'T FORGET MY FRIEND WHO BUYS EXTRA COOKED RICE WHEN HE ORDERS IN CHINESE FOOD.

In a wok or a cast-iron skillet, heat the oil and scramble the egg in it, on medium heat, stirring in the soy sauce. Add the celery, green onions and chicken, get everything acquainted, then stir in the rice and break it up, blending it into the mixture, and adding chicken stock—the amount depends on how moist you like your rice. It's kind of messy looking, but it tastes good.

Leftover Advice:

> If you made too much, stir it into some chicken broth for a rich soup.

CHICKEN AND MUSHROOMS

a few fresh mushrooms, sliced

a couple of green onions, snipped

3 tbsp (45 mL) chicken stock

1 cooked chicken breast, cut up

½ cup (125 mL) slivered almonds[12]

½ cup (125 mL) cooked rice

In a microwave dish, zap the mushrooms and green onions for 1 minute on Medium in 2 tbsp (25 mL) chicken stock. Stir in the chicken, almonds and rice, adding enough remaining chicken stock to moisten it all, and heat the mixture on High until piping. Fun to top it with a zingy plum sauce or something spicy, heating it for another half minute before you eat it.

Leftover Advice:

If you took the time to toast the almonds, and you burned them, melt some chocolate chips or a 1-oz square of semi-sweet chocolate (moistened with 1 tsp/5 mL milk—or butter) and stir in the nuts. This is for dessert. Don't burn them on purpose.

12 *IF YOU CAN SPARE THE TIME, TOAST THE ALMONDS, BUT WATCH THEM—THEY BURN EASILY: 2 MINUTES UNDER THE BROILER, STIRRING FREQUENTLY.*

TURKEY CHOW MEIN

1 or 2 chicken soup cubes OR 2 tbsp (25 mL) canned chicken broth

4 stalks celery, sliced

1 clove garlic, crushed

2 or 3 green onions, snipped

½ green pepper, chopped

½–1 cup (125–250 mL) cubed cooked
turkey breast

½ cup (125 mL) fresh or canned
mushrooms OR 1 can water chestnuts,
drained and sliced

1 can cream of celery soup

splash of soy sauce

1 cup (250 mL) chow mein noodles

In a microwave dish, soupée the celery, garlic,
onions and pepper just till friendly but still crisp—
about 1 minute on Medium-High. In a bowl, stir
together the turkey, mushrooms or water chestnuts,
celery soup and soy sauce. Stir in the vegetables. Put
the mixture back into the microwave dish, cover and
vent, and zap on Medium-High until it's hot—3 to 4
minutes—stirring and rotating once. Serve sprinkled with chow mein noodles.

Leftover Advice:

> One can of water chestnuts usually
> gives you more than you want.
> Save some of them for a spinach salad:
> raw spinach greens; 1 whole orange
> (peeled), cut up; a small red onion,
> sliced; and the water chestnuts, tossed
> with orange juice.

Most recipes for chicken are interchangeable with
turkey, but it's harder to find turkey breasts and
they're much bigger. Better to cook a turkey breast
for a special dinner (p. 213) and use leftover turkey
for some of these recipes. You can prepare the next
item with chicken or turkey as well, raw or cooked,
but this time ground up. Of course, the cooked meat
takes less time. The trick is to keep it moist enough.

CHICKEN (OR TURKEY) BURGER

4 oz (125 g) cooked or raw ground chicken or turkey

2 tbsp (25 mL) finely chopped onion

1 sloosh of Szechuan or teriyaki sauce OR ¼ cup (50 mL) low-fat yogurt

1 egg white, to bind it (optional)

seasoning to taste

1–2 tbsp (5–10 mL) chopped fresh coriander

2 tbsp (25 mL) peanuts, chopped

salt to taste

Gently mix everything together and form the meat into a burger patty.[13] Broil the patty in a toaster-oven for a couple of minutes on each side if the meat is already cooked, longer (4 minutes per side) if it's raw. It's dense meat; don't let it dry out. Baste it with additional Szechuan sauce if necessary. Serve on a bun or in pita bread with the desired condiments. I usually add a little more Szechuan sauce.

13 *IF YOU DO THIS AHEAD OF TIME AND MAKE SEVERAL PATTIES, BE SURE TO SEPARATE EACH PATTY WITH A DOUBLE LAYER OF WAXED PAPER BEFORE YOU PACKAGE AND FREEZE THEM.*

If you have trouble getting the cooked meat to stick together, roll it onto a little flour on your cutting board, one side and the other, and pat it into shape.

Not to forget summer, the last of the poultry is:

CHICKEN SALAD

> 1 cooked chicken breast, diced
>
> chopped celery, green onions, green pepper
>
> chopped almonds
>
> pineapple chunks OR canned mandarin oranges
>
> dressing, your choice, OR ½ cup (125 mL) yogurt, mixed with 1 tbsp (15 mL) mayo and salt to taste
>
> green grapes

Toss everything but the grapes gently, nestle into a lettuce leaf, garnish with the grapes, and pretend you're in a tea room.

I did promise you chicken livers.

CHICKEN LIVERS

> 1 or 2 frozen chicken soup cubes
>
> 1 onion, sliced
>
> 1 package chicken livers[14]
>
> 1 green pepper, cut into chunks

14 *TOO MUCH FOR ONE PERSON, BUT WHAT CHOICE DO YOU HAVE?*

In a wok or cast-iron skillet, soupée the onion quickly at high heat; add the chicken livers, stirring to brown them on all sides. Add the green peppers and cook a little longer—I like my livers rare. Serve at once on toast, with a salad.

Leftover Advice:

> There'll be cooked livers left over.
> Bring them back for a return engage-
> ment tossed with hot cooked fusilli and
> a few soupéed mushrooms and/or red
> pepper strips, warming this mixture in
> the microwave. (I add Szechuan sauce
> but that's because I'm addicted.) If
> there's still some left over, eat what you
> can, but be sure to eat all the peppers,
> and freeze the remains in a microwave
> dish. Repeat this recipe when you thaw
> it, adding fresh crisp peppers. Still one
> serving left? If the livers are as rare as I
> like them, process with a couple of
> green onions, freshly ground black pep-
> per and a splash of cognac to make an
> instant pâté. You can serve it with
> crackers to guests on the weekend or
> freeze it, but no longer than 4 weeks.[15]

15 *THE COGNAC HELPS THE LIVER SURVIVE REFREEZING AS PÂTÉ.*

WE'RE HAVING FISH THIS WEEK!

It's impossible for a single to use an entire package of frozen fish, but you have to thaw it anyway to release a serving-size piece, and by this time you're in for a fish feed. If you want easily separated fillets for one serving at a time, you pay more. So take some time on a Sunday and follow the package directions for thawing in the microwave. Once it's malleable, divide the fish, usually into four serving portions, which you will do something about right away and enjoy in luxury another day.

Because they've partially cooked in the thawing, they'll be even swifter to cook than usual. As to the kind of fish, when I shop the frozen food counter, I buy by price and adjust my taste buds. Most of these recipes will work with any fillets of haddock, perch, sole, blue fish and pollock.

The first recipe is one you can freeze and eat again.

FISH CHOWDER

> 1 potato, coarsely diced
>
> 1 onion, sliced
>
> 1 cup (250 mL) milk
>
> 1 portion of thawed fish, broken up
>
> real bacon bits
>
> freshly ground black pepper

Cook the potato[16] with the onion in the milk in a saucepan, being careful not to let the liquid boil over. When the potato is tender, add the fish and heat through. Stir in the bacon bits and pepper before serving. (I don't fry the bacon; you can buy real bacon bits, as opposed to imitation sawdust ones.) If the soup needs thinning, add more milk.

16 IF YOU'RE GOING TO HOLD ME TO THE FIVE-MINUTE LIMIT YOU HAVE TO START WITH A PRECOOKED POTATO.

That 10-minute fellow is as adamant about you having cooked potatoes on hand as I am about cooked rice. The fridge is getting crowded, but we already knew that.

Not Leftover Advice, but a nice touch:

> Do as they do in Bermuda and drop a little dark rum and some sherry peppers (or substitute Tabasco or Worcester-shire sauce) into your serving.

FISH FLORENTINE

1 portion of fish

buttermilk to cover

1 serving of cooked spinach

Parmesan cheese to taste

Zap the fish on Medium for 3 minutes in buttermilk to cover. In a small microwave dish, spread the fish over the cooked spinach and sprinkle with Parmesan cheese.

> **STOP HERE!**
> *You can wrap it up and freeze it until another time.*

Cover with vented plastic wrap and microwave for 4 to 5 minutes on Medium-High, turning the dish once. Let stand for a minute before you unwrap it.

Leftover Advice:

Remember what I told you about cooking the entire bag of spinach? Freeze the other serving immediately or save it for lunch tomorrow. If there's buttermilk-fish liquid left over, pour it into the fish chowder.

FISH CURRY

1 or 2 tbsp (15 or 25 mL) of chicken stock

1 onion, diced

curry powder, to taste

½–1 cup (125 to 250 mL) cooked rice

1 portion of thawed fish, cut into
chunks

pineapple chunks and juice

Put the chicken stock in a small microwave dish,
add the onion and sprinkle over the curry. Zap for
1 minute in the microwave on Medium. Stir in the
rice and fish, strew some pineapple casually around,
moisten with some of the juice and heat the mixture, covered and vented, in the microwave, 3 minutes. Let stand 1 minute, covered, before serving.

I was served a variation of this several times on a recent trip
to Iceland. It's a dish that allows for expansion.
Sometimes corn niblets were added to the mixture, some-
times grated cheese was sprinkled on top.
I'd put Major Grey Chutney on the side myself.

FISH BALLS

Every nation, it seems, has its own way of dealing
with cooked fish; gefilte fish comes to mind, and the
Icelandic *fiskur bollur*. Before the cod crisis, New-
foundlanders used to serve codfish balls, but the
balls are as scarce as the tongues now.

1 portion of thawed fish

salt and pepper

½ tsp (2 mL) chervil

1 egg white, to bind it

flour, to shape it

stock or white wine

Strictly speaking, you should start with raw fish and
grind it up, but there's a limit to your patience,

I know. Chop or grind the fish and mix it with the seasonings, the egg white and a little flour. Shape it into ping-pong-sized balls. Raw fish would be boiled in water for 10 minutes; your balls, requiring less time, can go into the microwave oven in a little stock or white wine, covered with wax paper, for 3 or 4 minutes on Medium. Let stand a minute and serve with pickled beets or beet horseradish. Into every life a little *chrain* must fall.[17]

17 THAT'S A PUN. **CHRAIN** IS BEET HORSERADISH.

> *Wet your hands with cold water to shape the mixture into balls that won't stick to you.*

FISH PILLOWS

Remember I told you about Girl Guide Cooking, aka Parchment Pillows? Here are four variations you can try with thawed fish. Take a piece of parchment paper, bigger than your piece of fish, and choose the following combinations (or make up your own):

1) 2 thin slices of Spanish onion
1 portion of thawed fish
fresh or dried dill
a couple of grinds of black pepper

2) 1 portion of thawed fish
2 big tbsp (25 mL) coriander pesto
(p. 186)

3) 1 portion of thawed fish
¼ cup (50 mL) salsa

4) 1 portion of thawed fish
2 tbsp (25 mL) light mayo,
with 1 clove garlic crushed into it

Spread the fish fillets lengthwise in a single layer on the parchment paper, in the first case laying them on top of the onion slices. Spread the suggested topping on the fish, covering the surface. Package the fish in a drugstore wrap, folding the ends under, and lay it in a microwave dish, venting the package in several places with a sharp knife. Microwave on Medium for 3 minutes. You're going to have to think fast to come up with an accompaniment. I suggest doing that before you zap the fish.

Mix ½ cup (125 mL) cooked rice with a handful of frozen peas in a microwave dish, drop in 1 frozen chicken soup cube and zap the mixture until heated, stirring once. Of course, you can do this in a saucepan on the stove.

Leftover Advice:

> If you have any leftovers, combine the fish with the rice mixture to reheat for lunch next day, maybe adding more peas or celery.

BAKED FISH PROVENÇALE

1 small onion, chopped

2 cloves garlic, crushed

1 tbsp (15 mL) oil OR 1 frozen chicken soup cube

1 small zucchini, chopped

½ green pepper, chopped

½ red pepper, chopped

1 tomato, chopped

black pepper

1 fillet fresh fish, preferably halibut

½ cup (125 mL) dry white wine

In a cast-iron skillet, sauté the onion and garlic in the oil or stock for about 1 minute at medium heat. Raise the heat and add the zucchini and peppers and perhaps a tad more moisture and cook another minute. Stir in the tomato, grind in some black pepper, and lay your portion of halibut gently over the vegetable mixture. Pour the white wine over the fish, cover the pan with foil and bake it in a regular oven for 20 to 25 minutes at 350°F (180°C). (If you want to transfer the vegetable mixture to a microwave dish, by all means do. Lay on the fish, pour in the wine, cover the dish with plastic wrap, vent, and cook for 7 to 10 minutes on Medium turning once. Leave it covered for 2 or 3 minutes before serving.)

If you can't find a piece of fresh halibut, then thaw an entire slab of fish and cook it all on the bed of vegetables, about 5 minutes in the microwave. Freeze the leftover portions.

SHRIMP PIG-OUT

1 serving frozen jumbo shrimp (6–10)[18]

1 bottle of beer

6 or 8 black peppercorns

In a saucepan, bring the beer to a boil with the peppercorns and drop the shrimp into it. Cook for 5 minutes, drain, rinse with cold water (to stop the cooking), and serve with salsa or aioli,[19] good bread and a finger salad (cherry tomatoes, green pepper sticks), so you can skip the cutlery. This is expensive, but you're worth it. The nice thing about being single is that expensive treats are sometimes affordable, and you don't have to share.

18 AT GREAT EXPENSE, YOU CAN BUY A BAG OF CLEANED FROZEN JUMBO SHRIMP. TAKE OUT AS MANY AS YOU WANT TO EAT AND KEEP THE REST IN THE FREEZER UNTIL FURTHER NOTICE. YOU CAN KEEP THEM FOR FOUR MONTHS, LONGER THAN YOU CAN RESIST THEM.

19 AIOLI IS A MAYONNAISE WITH CONVICTION: A WHOLE HEAD OF GARLIC, PEELED AND BLENDED WITH RAW EGG YOLKS, LEMON JUICE AND OIL, BUT I DARE NOT PASS THE RECIPE ON NOW BECAUSE OF THE THREAT OF

Leftover Advice:

> If I were you I'd save that fishy beer for fish chowder or bouillabaisse, but I know it's a responsibility you may not want to shoulder.

SALMONELLA. TRY BLENDING LIGHT MAYO WITH THE GARLIC AND SEE IF YOU LIKE THAT.

POLLOCK and RICE

People look down their noses at pollock because it's not crab and now, finally, it has stopped pretending to be. I like it, even in disguise. You can buy it frozen and undoctored and treat it like other frozen fish, but you can still buy the imitation crab stuff that people scoff at and do other things like sandwich filling or salad, or even something hot like this:

> 1 can (10 oz/284 mL) mushroom soup
>
> ¼ cup (50 mL) dry white wine
>
> ½ cup (125 mL) chopped celery
>
> ½ cup (125 mL) chopped mushrooms
>
> 1 serving of pollock pretending to be crab (4–6 oz/125-170 g)
>
> ½ cup (125 mL) cooked rice
>
> grated Parmesan cheese

Heat the soup, thinned with the wine, in a microwave bowl, then add the celery and mushrooms. Break up the pollock and stir it in. Put the rice in a microwave dish, pour the soup mixture over it, sprinkle with Parmesan cheese, cover and vent, and zap for 3 minutes on Medium. Serve with a salad or green beans.

Leftover Advice:

> You may have some of the liquid left over. Dump it in the fish chowder.

POLLOCK and BROCCOLI

If you're looking for something real Speed-Scratch, try this:

> 1 serving (4–6 oz/125-170 g) crab-flavoured pollock
>
> 1 can (10 oz/284 mL) broccoli-cheese soup
>
> 2 tbsp (25 mL) dry white wine
>
> ½ tsp (2 mL) dried tarragon
>
> ½ cup (125 mL) rice OR 1 serving linguine
>
> grated Parmesan cheese

Boil the linguine while you prepare the sauce. Thin the soup with wine, add the tarragon and stir in the pollock. Heat in the microwave (2 minutes on Medium) or in a saucepan. Serve over rice or linguine, sprinkled with the Parmesan cheese. (I admit, the linguine takes a little more time and another pot. Good, though.)

Leftover Advice:

> Pour any leftover sauce over a serving of cooked broccoli or cauliflower, adding a little grated cheese or/and a drop of sherry or Worcestershire sauce, and heat for lunch.

INDIVIDUAL MEAT LOAF

As I move into the beef mode, I might as well begin with meat loaf. Every single I spoke to had a special recipe for individual meat loaf. You probably have your own, too, so let's get this over with.

> 1 lb (500 g) lean ground beef
>
> ½ cup (125 mL) mixed oatmeal and oat bran
>
> 1 package dry onion soup mix OR 1 small onion, chopped, plus oregano, thyme, dry mustard
>
> 1 sloosh ketchup OR a little red wine OR beef stock (canned is fine)
>
> 1 egg white, to bind it
>
> freshly ground black pepper
>
> ¼ cup (50 mL) salsa

Dump all the ingredients except the salsa into a bowl and mix them well (bare hands are best). Shape the mixture into four loaves. Wrap three of them in plastic wrap and foil and freeze. Put tonight's dinner in a small microwave dish, cover it with wax paper and cook on High for 6 to 8 minutes, rotating after 3 minutes. Take off the wax paper, spread the salsa over the meat loaf and zap it on Medium for another minute. Let stand 5 minutes before serving—with oven-fried potatoes (see p. 49), since your microwave oven is busy, and a salad.

Leftover Advice:

> Bake it as one big loaf in the oven (1 hour at 350°F/180°C) and then you can have meat loaf sandwiches, which are only divine.

ONE LONE PATTY

4 oz (125 g) ground beef (a quarter-pounder!)

1 tbsp (15 mL) milk or 1 egg white, whichever comes first

1 clove garlic, minced

1 very small onion, finely chopped

seasonings to taste

Mix the meat with the milk, garlic, onions and seasonings and shape into a nice, round patty. Broil in the toaster-oven about 3 minutes per side, until rare but not oozing. Serve with everything your heart desires on a warmed hamburger bun, or Kaiser, or thick slice of French bread, or tuck it in a pita pocket. I like my salad with the meat: sliced tomatoes, lots of lettuce, sliced dill pickle.

WARNING

There's more danger out there. Don't eat any meat as rare as you used to but not too well done, either. And don't put cooked meat back on the plate where it stood raw; the blood will contaminate it.

Leftover Advice:

I'm a great believer in "as-you."[20] As you cook tonight's dinner, broil another patty or two and crumble the cooked meat into tomato sauce for a spaghetti sauce for another day. Season it later.

20 *AS YOU* DO SOMETHING, DO SOMETHING ELSE AT THE SAME TIME. NOT ALWAYS, OF COURSE. SOME THINGS DESERVE YOUR UNDIVIDED ATTENTION.

BACHELOR'S BEEF BY PEG BRACKEN

I am indebted to Peg Bracken for this next recipe—
the only one I have ever seen telling how to cook
roast beef for one person.

> 1 prime rib of beef, about 2 lb
> (just short of a kg)
>
> 1 clove garlic
>
> 2 baking potatoes, peeled

The trick in cooking this meat is to start with it
frozen, so bring it home, wrap it in foil and freeze it.
When you want to eat it, unwrap it, rub it all over
with a cut piece of garlic and put it on its side in a
small roasting pan, propped up with a peeled potato
on each side. Roast it at 400°F (200°C) for 1 hour
and 25 to 35 minutes, depending how rare you like it.
When you take it out of the oven, let it rest for 5 minutes before you slice it. The potatoes are good too.

Leftover Advice:

> This is certainly enough meat to share
> with a guest, or a child or two. If it's
> only you, then be happy, because the
> leftovers are delicious. Of course, roast
> beef sandwiches. And also a cooked
> version of steak tartare, if it's as rare as
> I think it is, processed with a few
> capers, an anchovy, a clutch of parsley,
> a small onion, a dash of cognac. Nice
> with garlic toast. But my favourite is the
> following, taken from Sardi's restaurant
> in New York.

DEVILLED BEEF BONES

1 egg

2 tbsp (25 mL) water

Worcestershire sauce

1 prime rib bone, with lots of meat on it

fresh bread crumbs

salt and pepper

Beat the egg, water and Wooster together with a fork and immerse the beef bone in it, getting it thoroughly wet. Then roll the bone around in seasoned bread crumbs, coating it thickly. Broil the bone 5 to 7 inches (12 to 18 cm) from the heat to allow it to get hot right through and toast the crumbs but not to burn them—about 10 minutes, turning. Serve with hot mustard, a glass of red wine and some good bread. Munch a few crudités before dinner so you don't have to bother with a salad. So you'll have no forks, one knife, just a few paper napkins. No one's watching, right?

Perhaps you'll find, as I do, that when you finally break down and broil a steak or roast a beast, you simply can't eat it all. Gone are the days of the man-killing (literally) 16-ounce Porterhouse falling off the sides of the plate. Even an 8-ounce steak is excessive these days; 4 ounces is quite sufficient. Strictly speaking, the following is a leftover recipe. So what if you do it on purpose?

STROGANOFF WITH VEGETABLES

2 cloves garlic, crushed

1 onion, sliced

1 frozen beef soup cube or canned beef broth OR the mushroom liquid OR ¼ cup (50 mL) red wine

4 oz (125 g) steak or roast beef, cooked (rare), cut in strips

1 can (10 oz/284 mL) or 1 cup (250 mL) sliced mushrooms

1 cup (250 mL) frozen mixed vegetables

1 tsp (5 mL) crushed dill seeds

½ cup (125 mL) low-fat sour cream

freshly ground black pepper

cooked noodles for one[21]

In a microwave dish, soupée the garlic and onion in the liquid and stir into a bowl with the steak strips, mushrooms and mixed vegetables. Heat in the microwave on Medium-High about 3 minutes, stirring once. Stir the dill seeds into the sour cream along with a generous grind of black pepper. Stir into the meat mixture and give it another minute in the microwave. Serve over cooked noodles.

21 *ON P. 95 I TOLD YOU HOW TO FREEZE LEFTOVER COOKED PASTA IN WATER. THIS WOULD BE A GOOD TIME TO HAUL IT OUT. PUT IT IN A STRAINER AND POUR BOILING WATER OVER IT, OR PUT IT ON HOLD IN A SAUCEPAN OF HOT WATER UNTIL YOU'RE READY FOR IT.*

CORNED BEEF HASH

Corned beef hash could well be classified as Comfort Food.

1 can corned beef

¼ cup (50 mL) ketchup or salsa

2 tbsp (25 mL) Dijon mustard

1 tbsp (15 mL) Worcestershire sauce

½ tsp (2 mL) dried basil

freshly ground black pepper to taste

1 cooked potato, diced[22]

1 or 2 frozen chicken soup cubes

1 clove garlic

½ cup (125 mL) grated Cheddar cheese (optional)

22 IF YOU DON'T HAVE A COOKED POTATO IN THE FRIDGE (THERE ARE LIMITS, I KNOW), THEN PEEL AND DICE ONE AND PUT IT IN A MICROWAVE DISH WITH THE GARLIC TO COOK ON HIGH IN THE CHICKEN CUBES, COVERED AND VENTED, FOR 2 TO 4 MINUTES. USE WHEN CALLED FOR.

Break the beef into a cast-iron pan spritzed with the merest bit of oil, over medium heat. Stir in the ketchup, mustard, Wooster, basil and pepper and cook and stir until the beef gets nice and oozy. Stir in the cooked potatoes and garlic, increase heat to high and cook until the bottom gets golden and crusty. With a spatula, carefully flip the hash and do the other side. Dump it out onto a plate to serve. You could top the mess with grated cheese and slip it under the broiler but I think this is fat enough as it is.

Leftover Advice:

It's a great leftover, if there is any, because it ripens.

PORK CHOP PILLOW[23]

Here's another prize from my Girl Guide Cooking Exploration: a successful, speedy parchment package.

23 KNOWING THE THEORY, KNOWING IT WORKS, YOU MIGHT CONTINUE TO EXPLORE THIS PARCHMENT COOKING ON YOUR OWN. I CERTAINLY INTEND TO.

1 small onion, sliced

freshly ground black pepper

1 butterflied pork chop, no more than ½ inch (1 cm) thick

1 sweet potato, peeled and thinly sliced

Szechuan sauce

On top of a large piece of parchment paper spread a layer of onion slices the same size as the pork chop. Grind black pepper over the onions and place the chop on top of them. Cover the chop with one layer of sweet potato slices. (Because the chop is butterflied, it covers a larger area; you won't go short of potato.) Pour a little Szechuan sauce over the potatoes, then wrap up the parcel with a drugstore wrap, tucking the end flaps under it as you place it in a microwave dish. Vent each side with a sharp knife and then zap it on High for 4 minutes. Amazing! It's cooked, tender, and dinner fit for a single. Serve it with spinach.

No Leftover Advice, unless you count the unsliced portion of sweet potato. Roast it with some other lonely veg (p. 207)

HAZEL'S QUICK-RETURN MEAL[24]

For those days when even Speed-Scratch is beyond you, here's something from a smart woman who made it in the stock market.

"Walk to the freezer cabinets in your favorite grocery store. Pick out a yummy-looking meal in a box. Take to checkout counter. Head for home and pop it in the microwave oven. Enjoy!"

24 *BEARDSTOWN LADIES, DOO-DAH, DOO-DAH.*

PART TWO

Meatless Dinner Recipes

*I think if the vegetables controlled the
world there would be enough for all,
since even a vegetable knows its duty is
to feed the earth.*

~ Tom Wayman

A lot of people these days are eating less meat, if
any, and fewer eggs, as anyone who watches TV
commercials knows. In addition to a spate of vegetarian cookbooks, there are ones labelled *almost*
vegetarian for consumers who eat a little chicken, a
little fish and a lot of pasta and who want to be
introduced to the magic world of legumes. The following recipes are for those who prefer to go meatless—all the time or once in a while.

The low-fat kick has put on the grains and
legume circuit people who didn't really expect or
intend to be. "The Diet Your Doctor Won't Give
You," prepared by the Women's National Health
Network in the U.S., was published by *Ms* magazine
in 1987 and dropped the first hints of how to cut

down on fat—grams, not avoirdupois. Several years later, to my surprise, my own doctor recommended reducing the number of fat grams I ingested. That's when I discovered that if I was really going to be serious about cutting down on fat, the first thing that had to be drastically reduced was my consumption of red meat. That's how I came so late in life to a whole new world of cooking and taste sensations.

"I can't believe what I'm eating!" I say as I sit down to dine on curried lentils and rice or quinoa salad.[24] At an age when I should be making the tried-and-true recipes I have lived with all my life and could make with my eyes closed—all the '50s-style food of my early married days when I was learning about life and love and gelatin salads—I have been making new discoveries and tossing out old recipes and ideas, not to say prejudices.

I was always an adventurous cook: I introduced myself and my friends to artichokes, quiche, crudités and Cherries Jubilee. They sound like ho-hum clichés now, in the light of our worldly, cosmopolitan consciousness. In those unsophisticated days I hadn't even heard of guacamole; no one had, not where I lived. Tabbouleh, couscous, hummus, polenta, salsa, pesto, tahini—all this delicious food I'd never heard of when I was 20—I'm cooking and eating now, and loving it. It's not only the expanding awareness about fat that has worked this miracle, it is the shrinking of the world. Now as never before we have not only the riches of the earth available in the supermarket—although I must admit that some markets are more super than others—but also the knowledge of how other people live and what they eat. Given enough time to digest all this new information, we may even learn to understand each other.

24 LAWK-A-MERCY-ON-ME, THIS IS NONE OF I.

182

Take pasta, something we all know. We wallow in the pleasures of pasta, staid, stolid, sturdy Canadians that we are, all absolutely (pine) nuts over pasta. Entire cookbooks abound devoted to nothing but pasta. Pasta machines are selling like hot capellini, but if you don't already have one, don't rush out because it really doesn't pay a single to make pasta on the premises. Treasure the name of your neighbourhood pasta pusher, or read your labels.

Like other carbohydrates about to be canonized, pasta used to be verboten—too fattening. Even Weight Watchers allows carefully measured pasta now, as a bread exchange. Gourmet cooks recommend it to lovers as an *après amour* snack in bed,[25] as a wonderful vehicle for chèvre[26] and as an effective way to impress other people with your spelling skills.[27]

25 WATCH HOW YOU USE THAT FORK!

26 GOAT CHEESE IS IN BECAUSE IT HAS A RELATIVELY LOW FAT CONTENT.

27 THIS IS GOING TO TEST MY SPELL-CHECK TO THE LIMIT.

A WORD ABOUT BUYING PASTA
Make sure it's made with durum wheat flour to guarantee a firm product. Whole wheat is even better for you.

If you didn't know it already: there is more to pasta than spaghetti. There are gnocchi, which some people call dumplings but which classify as pasta; cannelloni—Italian crêpes; capelletti, also spelled capoletti—sort of Italian kreplach; capelli—very thin noodles; capelini—small, very thin noodles; cavatelli—a long, crinkle-edged shell; farfalle—bows; fettuccine—you all know this one; fusilli—corkscrews; lasagna; linguine; and don't forget all the noodles with eggs in them, to say nothing of macaroni, manicotti, maruzelle—more shells; orzo—which looks like rice; penne—short tubes; ravioli; spaghetti, of course—it means little strings;

spaghettini—littler strings; tagliarini—very narrow egg noodles; tagliatelle—wide, flat egg noodles; vermicelli—translates as worms; and ziti—bridegrooms; not to mention cellophane noodles, chow mein, spaetzle, udon noodles and angel hair. If I've missed your favourite, don't tell me.

There's fresh pasta, to be purchased from your favourite pasta maker, stored in the fridge and used within a week; it takes a little less time to cook. Dry pasta (durum wheat, remember) keeps well on the shelf, so storage can be a problem if you indulge in a variety of shapes.[28]

Contemporary pasta makers put spinach, tomatoes and other things in their pasta dough—even chocolate—all of which, but not all together, add colour, vitamins and taste. Whole wheat or buckwheat flour make the pasta look muddy when cooked but give you more fibre.

The emphasis is, however, on the sauce, and this is where you have to be careful. As with potatoes, it's not the pasta that does you in, calorie-wise, it's what you put on top. If you're thinking red as in tomato, good as it is, you are behind the times. Be aware that there are lower-fat ways to make the Big Red and some of them involve no meat. Baby carrots instead of meatballs are a delicious surprise. If you're thinking white as in cream sauce, you are in Fat City, so be careful: all that butter, all that cream! I'm rhapsodic about stir-fry these days, tossed with pasta, no sauce at all, just lots of wonderful taste.

Whatever you choose to put on your pasta, did you know that it raises your morale? I read that certain carbohydrates tend to make the consumer euphoric. Here I thought it was just me and the garlic. That remains the simplest of all seasonings

28 *IT'S NOT MERELY A MATTER OF AESTHETICS, WHICH PASTA YOU THINK IS MOST ATTRACTIVE LOOKING. SOME SHAPES TAKE BETTER TO SOME SAUCES. FUSILLI, FOR EXAMPLE, LURES TASTE INTO EVERY CONVOLUTION. GO AHEAD AND EXPERIMENT.*

for pasta: garlic and oil. Actually, garlic is not a seasoning, it's a mind set.[29] By a natural association, this brings me to pesto.

Pesto is very popular with pasta and turns out to be one of the missing elements in my body that I have to replenish frequently or die. The first time I ever made pesto, for a pistou (Provençale soup) recommended by Julia Child, I used dried basil, not knowing a thing about the uses of the fresh herb. Now I am addicted to it. I grow it in the summer and call myself fortunate that the squirrels don't like it. In the off-season I buy it in fresh clumps in big-city stores. My first meal at home after I've been away is pasta with an awesome pesto: fresh basil and about eight cloves of garlic, to start my fire going again. But it can be expensive. I mean, have you checked the price of pine nuts lately? I will offer a few other versions of pesto that you will find easier on the pocketbook and almost as addictive. Yes, I'm going to share my pesto with you.[30]

> **QUICK TIP (Not to say, a nag)**
> If you're planning on pasta for dinner, start the water boiling the minute you come in the door. That way, you'll come in on the 10-minute mark—the average length of time it takes pasta to cook.

PASTA WITH PESTO

Basil Pesto

7 or 8 cloves garlic

about 1 cup (250 mL) fresh basil leaves[31]

2 tbsp (25 mL) grated Parmesan cheese

29 I HAD FRIENDS IN THE DIPLO-MATIC CORPS WHOSE FIRST POST-ING WHEN THEY MARRIED WAS TO MANILA. THEY WERE TOLD TO STAKE OUT A DOCTOR AND KEEP CHECKING SO THEY WOULDN'T BE INVADED WITH SOME PARASITE FOR LIFE. THEIR DOCTOR, A DELIGHTFUL LITTLE GERMAN JEW, ADVISED THEM TO EAT GARLIC A MINIMUM OF ONCE A WEEK AS THE BEST HEALTH PRESERVATIVE THEY COULD FIND. SPAGHETTI CON AGLIO ED OLIO IS THE SIMPLEST WAY A GARLIC LOVER COULD DIE AND ALREADY BE IN HEAVEN: GARLIC AND OLIVE OIL AND BLACK PEPPER, AND MAYBE A SCINTILLA OF CHOPPED PARSLEY. (MERELY SAYING IT IS FUN, TOO.)

30 THERE ARE VERY FEW PEOPLE I DO THIS FOR AND YOU'RE SOME OF THE FEW.

31 I'M SUCH AN ACCEPTING PERSON, I TAKE WHAT'S GIVEN/SOLD TO ME. MOSTLY IT'S JUST A BUNCH, AND I ALWAYS TRIM OFF ALL THE

¼ cup (50 mL) or less olive oil

2 tbsp (25 mL) pine nuts

Drop the peeled garlic into the mini-processor first and give it a whirl, chopping it up very fine. Wash and spin-dry the basil before you stuff it in the bowl but don't worry if it's damp. You're using less oil than is usually called for, so you can welcome the moisture. Drop the cheese on top of the basil, put the lid on and turn on the motor. With the motor on, pour olive oil through the chimney until the mixture looks about right.[32] Remove the lid and test it, scraping down the bowl and turning the mixture over to be sure all the leaves get scrunched. Whirl again (lid on), then drop in the pine nuts and give them a go-round but not too much because you want to retain their texture.

Spoon this mixture onto the hot pasta of your choice, tossed with a modicum of oil to help ooze the pesto around.

Leftover Advice:

The pesto keeps in the fridge for a few days and you can drop it into soup and onto anything you think needs a lift. If you're going away, freeze it in a tightly covered container and use it as soon as you return.

Parsley Pesto

Parsley Pesto is cheaper than Basil Pesto.

1–2 cups (250–500 mL) packed parsley, stems removed, washed and spun

STEMS OF BASIL, CORIANDER, DILL OR WATERCRESS (SPINACH, TOO). MOST OF THESE BUNCHES PACK DOWN TO ABOUT A CUP WHEN I SHOVE THEM INTO MY MINI-PROCESSOR.

32 *LOOKS AND TASTES. IT LOOKS LIKE GREEN SLUDGE BUT THE OIL AND THE PARMESAN MAKE IT AMENABLE TO THE HEAT OF THE PASTA. I GUESS IT'S ABOUT THE VISCOSITY OF OATMEAL PORRIDGE.*

2 cloves garlic

4 tbsp (50 mL) grated Emmenthal cheese

¼ cup (50 mL) or less olive oil

2 tbsp (25 mL) sunflower seeds

Same method.

Spinach Pesto

If the spinach is coarse, try partially cooking it in its own moisture for about 2 minutes on high heat, turning a couple of times, before you drain it and blend it.

1 bag fresh spinach, stems removed, washed and spun

4 cloves garlic

½ cup (125 mL) grated Parmesan cheese

¼ cup (50 mL) or less olive oil

4 tbsp (50 mL) sunflower seeds

Same method.

Coriander Pesto

1–2 cups (250–500 mL) packed coriander, stems removed, washed and spun

5 cloves garlic

¼ cup (50 mL) or less olive oil

handful of peanuts

Same method. This is also great added to soup.

PASTA PRIMAVERA

2 frozen chicken soup cubes OR a spritz of oil

1 clove garlic, crushed

4 green onions, snipped

1 red pepper, cut in strips

1 serving broccoli, tender-crisp, OR asparagus, ditto, OR cauliflowerets, ditto, OR a combination of the above

a mittful of fresh basil or fresh parsley

couple of grinds of black pepper

1 serving cooked penne

grated Parmesan cheese

Soupée the garlic and onions in a wok or cast-iron skillet at medium heat until convivial and add the pepper strips. Stir in the broccoli to heat. Dance in the basil or parsley, be judicious with the pepper. Toss in the drained penne and mingle. Be lavish with the Parmesan on serving.

Leftover Advice:

The above is not Speed-Scratch, it *is* leftover.

ASPARAGUS AND FUSILLI

1 serving fusilli

2 frozen vegetable or chicken soup cubes OR a spritz of oil

3 green onions, snipped

1 serving asparagus, cut in inch-lengths

fresh parsley, trimmed and snipped

freshly ground black pepper

½ cup (125 mL) grated mozzarella cheese (or Lappi, which is lower fat)

While you cook the fusilli in your ever-ready boiling water, soupée the onions in a cast-iron skillet at medium heat. Add the asparagus and cook quickly. Add the parsley and black pepper to taste. Add the drained fusilli, toss with the cheese and serve immediately.

For Speedier Scratch, toss the drained fusilli with 1 serving of frozen mixed designer veg. It cooks as it heats. Add cheese and voilà! *If it's cool in your pasta bowl, just zap it for a minute.*

Leftover Advice:

No leftovers from this, but if you don't have any fresh ingredients to stir into the pasta, make do with your pantry. For example, abuse a cooking onion in stock, then toss in artichoke hearts, black olives and oregano; or canned Romano beans, tomato sauce and jalapeños; or anchovies and garlic; or lemon juice, garlic and oil, nice if you have some cream…When in doubt, improvise.

MUSHROOMS AND TARRAGON

1 serving linguine

1 frozen vegetable or frozen chicken
soup cube OR a spritz of oil

2 green onions, snipped

1 cup (250 mL) sliced fresh mushrooms[33]

½ tsp (2 mL) dried tarragon

¼ cup (50 mL) low-fat sour cream

33 YOU COULD MAKE THIS RECIPE
    WITH CANNED MUSHROOMS, BUT
    FRESH ARE BETTER.

Boil the linguine and don't start cooking this one
until your pasta is almost ready to serve, because
mushrooms are very swift. In a cast-iron skillet
soupée the green onions on medium-high, add the
mushrooms and cook quickly, stirring gently. Add
the tarragon and stir in the sour cream. When it's
hot—but don't boil it—spoon it over the drained
pasta.

ABOUT MUSHROOMS
*Button mushrooms are the most common; they release a lot
of liquid when cooked—drain if necessary.
Oyster mushrooms are very mild, so spike 'em up.
Dried porcini are expensive, so enjoy—with garlic and oil,
with rice or pasta. Shiitakes absorb rather than release
liquid, and get plump and juicy.*

Leftover Advice:

If you have some of this left over,
pull some cooked chicken livers out of
the freezer (p. 163) and mix this in
with them. Reheat in the microwave
for dinner tomorrow night.

34 THIS IS A STRIPPED-DOWN
VERSION OF PASTA NINOTCHKA,
THE FAVOURITE NAME FOR IT.
BEING SINGLE, YOU CAN ENJOY IT
AFTER A PARTY WHEN THERE'S
ONLY ENOUGH FOR YOU.

RUSSIAN PASTA[34]

1 serving fettuccine

a smidge of olive oil

1 tbsp (15 mL) lumpfish caviar

black pepper

1 or 2 slices smoked salmon, cut up

Cook the fettuccine in boiling water until tender, about 10 minutes, then drain and toss gently in the oil. Stir in the roe, pepper and salmon, and be grateful you're single.

ENOUGH RED PEPPERS[35]

1 serving fusilli

1 frozen vegetable or chicken soup cube OR a spritz of oil

2 or 3 cloves garlic

2 red peppers, cut in ½-inch (1 cm)-wide strips

generous grating of Parmesan cheese (even better with Asiago)

While the pasta is boiling, soupée the garlic in the oil in a wok or cast-iron skillet at medium heat. Raise the heat and add the red peppers and cook quickly. Add the drained fusilli and toss and stir-fry. Serve at once topped with the cheese.

PASTA WITH TOMATO SAUCE

Some of the commercial bottled pasta sauces are delicious, especially the meatless ones, and save a lot of time. I recommend them

In the summer, if you're fortunate enough to have a garden or foolhardy enough to have bought a whole basket of fresh tomatoes,[36] why not make your own

36 NOT REALLY LEFTOVERS BUT OVERAGE—A BLUSH OF TOMATOES?

SPAGHETTI SAUCE?

Peel the tomatoes (2 quarts/2 L), if you're up to it, otherwise drop them quartered into a stock pot with about 4 cloves garlic, crushed, 1 large onion, diced, maybe some old green pepper, cut up, a sloosh of ketchup or ½ cup (125 mL) of tomato juice or salsa or something red, plus a small can of tomato paste, and the heel of a bottle of red wine. Add 1 tsp (5 mL) each salt, dried oregano and Worcestershire sauce, several good grinds of black pepper and a couple of small bay leaves. Start the heat gently to see how much liquid the tomatoes release. (They should be pretty wet.) When the sauce is bubbling nicely, turn the heat down, cover the pot, and simmer on low for at least an hour or until it thickens nicely. Cool, remove the bay leaves, and freeze in portions to suit you. When you thaw and heat the sauce, you could drop in some sliced fresh mushrooms and a handful of baby carrots as it's warming.

LINGUINE WITH CHÈVRE

1 serving linguine

1 cup (250 mL) low-fat yogurt

1 small fistful of chèvre

4 cloves garlic, crushed

While you wait for the linguine to cook in boiling water, heat the yogurt in the top of a double boiler over hot water. Crumble in the goat cheese to melt it and stir in the garlic. Toss this mixture in the linguine, top with Parmesan if you must, and don't breathe on anyone.

> *This might be a good time to sieve the sauce so there are no lumps of garlic. You want **smooth**.*

Leftover Advice:

Any leftover sauce can be poured on asparagus or broccoli tomorrow, or puréed with cooked cauliflower for a fast soup, or thickened with light mayo for a vegetable dip.

CABBAGE AND NOODLES

1 serving noodles

2 frozen vegetable or chicken soup cubes OR a spritz of oil

1 medium onion, diced

1 cup (250 mL) coarsely shredded cabbage

2 tbsp (25 mL) low-fat yogurt OR
Szechuan sauce[37]

37 *MY CHOICE, BUT I'M TRYING TO
BE BROAD-MINDED ABOUT THIS.*

2 tbsp (25 mL) caraway seeds

Cook the noodles in boiling water and while they
are cooking, soupée the onion on high heat, stir in
the cabbage and cook over high heat just until tender-crisp. Stir in the noodles, the yogurt and caraway
seeds and mingle gently. Serve at once.

Leftover Advice:

I know that cabbage seems to expand to
fill the space allotted to it. Leftovers in
this case are easily taken care of the
next day because it's so good you'll eat
it all up. See Cabbage (p. 41) for other
suggestions. And see also Japanese
Quinoa Salad (p. 200).

NOODLE FRITTATA

1 frozen vegetable or chicken soup
cube OR a spritz of oil

1 tbsp (15 mL) diced onion

2 tbsp (25 mL) chopped green pepper

½ cup (125 mL) leftover cooked noodles

1 egg, lightly beaten

¼ cup (50 mL) grated Parmesan or
mozzarella cheese

¼ cup (50 mL) sunflower seeds
(optional)

freshly ground black pepper

In a cast-iron skillet, soupée the onion and green pepper on medium-high until soft, stir in the noodles and egg and stir-fry until the noodles are coated, adding the cheese and sunflower seeds at will. (You really have something more like egg-fried noodles rather than a frittata. It tastes better than it looks.) Top with black pepper and serve at once.

> **COMFORTING NOODLES**
> Cook 1 serving of noodles and load them up with salt and soft butter that melts on meeting their warmth. So will you.

TORTELLINI

Buy packaged cheese-filled tortellini, cook them all and eat half, tossed with pesto, served with a salad. Store the remainder in the fridge and reheat them in a little chicken stock in the microwave with more pesto.

I know I gave you a pasta salad for lunch, but here's another one to consider for dinner:

SUMMER PASTA SALAD

1 cup (250 mL) cooked macaroni

lots of chopped fresh salad vegetables, including celery and red and green pepper

1 tsp (5 mL) caraway seeds, crushed

½ cup (125 mL) buttermilk, lightly salted, OR light Ranch Dressing

The hard part is limiting the amount of material you're working with to keep the serving suitable for a small army. All I can say is, be careful, be discreet, and if you get carried away, then toss it out before it claims squatter's rights in your fridge.

In the various informal surveys I have conducted, many singles who do not otherwise cook much cook pasta. Most of them, however, unless they are already vegetarian, do not take the lateral step to legumes and grains, being unaware of the rewards to their health, taste buds, pocketbook and figure. Vegetarians are usually thinner than carnivores, and I don't know anyone who minds being thinner. Look at George Bernard Shaw and Mahatma Gandhi, also Darryl Hannah, as examples of vegetarians, for whatever comfort it gives you.

I know I've advised you to try to have cooked brown rice in your fridge for chicken emergencies or plans. So I'll give you something else to plan to use it on.

MUSHROOM FRIED RICE

    1 egg

    1 tbsp (15 mL) oil

    2 tsp (10 mL) hoisin sauce

    2 stalks celery, thinly sliced

    3 green onions, snipped

    ½ cup (125 mL) sliced fresh mushrooms

    1 cup (250 mL) cooked brown rice

    chicken or vegetable stock to taste

    nuts (optional)

In a wok or cast-iron skillet, scramble the egg in the oil on medium-high heat and stir in the hoisin sauce. Add the celery and green onions, give them a moment to get acquainted and then add the mushrooms, stirring them until they're coated and warm. Stir in the rice and break it up, blending it into the mixture, and adding stock depending on how moist you like your rice. You might like to strew some nuts on top, for fun.

Leftover Advice:

> Don't laugh, but this is quite good on toast with extra hoisin sauce, or roll it up in a tortilla and call it delicious.

BASIC RISOTTO

Risotto is rice with a difference; it takes more forethought, also more time. Think of it as a Sunday afternoon well spent.

2 tbsp (25 mL) oil

1 green onion, snipped very fine

1 cup (250 mL) long grain white rice

2 tbsp (25 mL) white wine

2 cups (500 mL) hot chicken broth

2 pinches powdered saffron[38]

38 I KNOW SAFFRON IS EXPENSIVE, BUT THERE REALLY ISN'T ANY WAY TO DUPLICATE THE TASTE. IF YOU CAN'T DO IT, THEN HEAT 1 TBSP (15 ML) GOOD CURRY POWDER IN 1 TSP (5 ML) HOT WATER AND USE THAT.

In a saucepan, heat the oil and sauté the onion over medium-low heat until it's soft. Stir in the rice and cook-stir until it's well and truly coated with the oil. Raise the heat and add the wine, stirring until it disappears. Now stir in about 1 cup (250 mL) of broth. Cover and cook until the broth is absorbed, but watch it and stir the rice once in a while. When the liquid has been absorbed, add another cup of broth and keep watch, stirring. When the rice is cooked through it looks almost creamy; this takes up to half an hour, breaking all my rules. Add the saffron dissolved in 1 tsp (5 mL) hot water. Serve as a heavenly side dish with chicken or fish, or give it top billing with the treat of a fresh artichoke. Keep black pepper at hand to grind, and maybe some grated Parmesan cheese.

Leftover Advice:

See the following recipes.

RISOTTO WITH MUSHROOMS

6–8 mushrooms, sliced

¼ cup (50 mL) lemon juice

1 serving leftover risotto

lots of grated Parmesan, Romano, or Asiago cheese

Toss the sliced mushrooms in lemon juice and zap on Medium for 2 minutes. Drain and stir into leftover risotto, reheated in a little chicken broth. More cheese, please.

CURRIED RISOTTO

a spritz of oil

maybe 1 tbsp (15 mL) curry powder

1 apple, peeled, cored and chopped

1 small onion, chopped

1 small zucchini, sliced (optional)

combination or choice of:
   2 tbsp (25 mL) sunflower seeds
   2 tbsp (25 mL) peanuts, chopped
   1 tbsp (15 mL) sesame seeds

1 serving leftover risotto or cooked
brown rice

If you're not starting with a curry-based rice, then stir the curry into the oil as it heats in a skillet. Over medium-high heat add the apple, onion and zucchini and stir-fry until softened but still textured. Stir in the nuts or seeds and the rice and heat through.

Leftover Advice:

If this is too much for you, reheat the next day for lunch, and if it's not enough, add a sliced tomato and banana on the side.

Here's a lovely thing to do with rice:

EGGPLANT AND RED PEPPER ON RICE

1 serving cooked rice

1 medium eggplant[39]

1 large red pepper

2 or 3 frozen chicken or vegetable soup cubes

lots of grated Parmesan or Asiago cheese

39 *EGGPLANT TENDS TO ABSORB ALL THE OIL YOU CAN GIVE IT. THE NICE THING ABOUT THIS RECIPE IS YOU DON'T GIVE IT ANY OIL AT ALL.*

Warm the rice in the microwave, 2 minutes on Medium-High with a little chicken soup to moisten if necessary. Peel and slice the eggplant lengthwise and cut into strips about an inch wide; cut the red pepper into strips of the same width. Zap the vegetables in a microwave dish in a couple of soup cubes, stirring and shifting once or twice, for 5 or 6 minutes on Medium until tender. Lay a suitable amount of the vegetables across the warm rice, sprinkle lavishly with the cheese and zap again, or broil until the cheese is oozy.

To release the bitterness of eggplant, lay the slices on a platter and salt generously. Cover with waxed paper and a weight and let it sweat for half an hour. Pour off the liquid before you cook it.

Leftover Advice:

If you can't eat all of this, pick out the red peppers and put them in any rice or stir-fry dish you are planning soon. Make a hero sandwich with the remaining eggplant: layer it on a slice of toasted focaccia bread with grilled red onion slices and grated cheese. Broil and eat for lunch or supper.

RICE AND BLACK BEANS

1 cup (250 mL) cooked rice

1 (14 oz/398 mL) can black beans, drained

2 tbsp (25 mL) minced jalapeño peppers

1 red pepper, chopped

grated cheese, your choice

Combine all the ingredients except the cheese, moistening if necessary with a little chicken or vegetable stock. Ladle one serving into a microwave dish, sprinkle with cheese, and zap for 2 or 3 minutes on Medium, stirring at least once.

Leftover Advice:

> The remaining mixture can be apportioned in single servings and frozen in microwave dishes. Keeps up to 2 months. Thawing takes about 4 minutes in the microwave, with stirring. Add the cheese and heat for one more minute.

I think the biggest discovery of my new life with food is quinoa. It's one of the oldest grains known and offers the most complete protein of any grain.

> *TO PREPARE QUINOA:*
>
> *Wash in a strainer under warm running water for 3 minutes. Cook in boiling salted water to cover for 7 to 10 minutes, then drain and use as you please.*

JAPANESE QUINOA SALAD

2 cups (500 mL) cooked quinoa

2 or 3 green onions, snipped

1 wedge of cabbage, finely sliced

2 tbsp (25 mL) sesame seeds, toasted

½ cup (125 mL) sliced mushrooms

3 stalks celery, sliced diagonally

¼ cup (50 mL) sunflower seeds or slivered almonds

Dressing:

¼ cup (50 mL) or less olive oil

1 tbsp (15 mL) soy sauce

1 tbsp (15 mL) lemon juice

1 tbsp (15 mL) brown sugar

1 tsp (5 mL) grated fresh ginger

Shake the dressing ingredients together in a small jar. Combine the salad ingredients and toss with the dressing, chill for an hour to ripen, and eat.

Leftover Advice:

Cooked quinoa can just as easily be served as a cereal with raisins, honey, chopped apples, whatever. It's grain, after all.

So is bulgur—wheat, actually, and best known to us Westerners in the now classic salad called tabbouleh.[40]

TABBOULEH

You don't have to go through the soaking-in-boiling-water routine with bulgur now. Tabbouleh mixes are available in the supermarkets with seasoning and directions. All you have to do is add the extras at your discretion.

bulgur, from a mix

1 tomato, chopped

½ cucumber, chopped

1 tsp (5 mL) mint—dried is okay but fresh is better

40 A FEW YEARS AGO I HAD A DINNER PARTY THAT INCLUDED A FAMILY OF CANADIANS HOME ON LEAVE FROM IRAN. I HAD PLANNED ON GRILLED TURKEY BREAST AND TABBOULEH FOR THE ADULTS AND SOMETHING SIMPLER FOR THE CHILDREN. WHILE I WAS SETTING OUT THE FOOD, THE FOUR-YEAR-OLD BOY CAME OUT TO THE KITCHEN TO SEE WHAT I WAS DOING AND SPOTTED THE SALAD. "TAB-BOULEH!" HE SHOUTED WITH HOME-SICK ENTHUSIASM. "OH, BOY—TABBOULEH!!"

IT PROVES MY POINT, THAT IT'S ALL IN WHAT YOU GET USED TO.

Prepare the bulgur according to the package directions and stir in the tomato, cucumber and mint.

Really a side dish, good with turkey breast (see p. 213), but if you're choosing meatless, serve it as a side dish with a vegetable-laden couscous.

COUSCOUS

Couscous is another grain that used to take more time to prepare than it does now. Billed as the Moroccan pasta, couscous is ready in 7 minutes for whatever you want to add to it.

> 1 serving couscous, prepared according to package directions (about 1 cup (250 mL))

Stir into the hot couscous, according to your desire and your pantry shelves:

> artichoke hearts, drained, and/or chick peas, drained
>
> black pepper
>
> OR:
>
> a handful of raisins
>
> a handful of sunflower seeds
>
> pinch of cinnamon
>
> OR:
>
> 1 green pepper, cut in chunks
>
> 2 or 3 stalks celery, ditto
>
> couple of green onions, snipped
>
> leftover cooked vegetables[41]

41 IF YOU'RE NOT AVERSE TO IT, I'D SUGGEST SOME LEFTOVER MEAT: COOKED CHICKEN OR TURKEY, CHICKEN LIVERS, MAYBE EVEN LAMB.

Leftover Advice:

> If the prepared couscous looks like too much for you to handle, save part of it, undoctored, and eat it for breakfast heated in the microwave with maple syrup and raisins. If you're reheating it for dinner consumption, moisten it with some chicken stock.

Legumes[42] have a high protein content, though not nearly as much fat as red meat[43] and they're much cheaper than meat. You've heard of chick peas, lima beans and navy, also lentils, split peas, peanuts and soybeans, but this is just the tip of the iceberg. There are more than 11,000 species of legumes—but they're not all available in your local supermarket, and few of them pass the five-minute test unless they're already cooked and canned. I love to go to a really cosmopolitan farmers' market to revel in the beans for sale. Still, there's more variety in the canned ones than there used to be.

Here's something nice to do with black beans:

BLACK BEAN SALAD

> 1 serving black beans
>
> 1 serving roasted red peppers (p. 68)
>
> 3 stalks celery, chopped
>
> 1 tbsp (15 mL) capers, chives or chopped parsley in
>
> ¼ cup (50 mL) light vinaigrette (p. 87)

Combine all the ingredients and allow to rest and ripen—in the fridge, overnight or all day. Serve chilled or at room temp.

42 *BEANS TO YOU.*

43 *ONE CUP OF WHITE, LIMA OR KIDNEY BEANS, CHICK PEAS OR LENTILS HAS 1 GRAM OF FAT; SOYBEANS HAVE 16; A LOT OF BEEF AND LAMB IS IN THE TEENS AND LOW 20S.*

If you're opening a lot of these beans and such, save all the juice they come in for vegetable broth. Freeze it in cubes, like chicken stock, and use it for cooking.

Leftover Advice:
Mush any leftovers in the processor and use like refried beans. Spread on nachos, topped with cheese and zapped until oozy.

Here's an odd but good one:

KIDNEY BEAN SALAD

1 can (14 oz/398 mL) kidney beans, drained

1 cup (250 mL) pineapple chunks

4 stalks celery, chopped

2 tbsp (25 mL) diced jalapeños

tight fistful of fresh cilantro, snipped

Toss this combination gently with some of the pineapple juice and chill for a while to ripen.

Leftover Advice:
Stir some leftover cooked rice into this and heat it for a satisfying dinner. If it needs more moistening, you have lots of veggie broth.

How can we mention kidney beans without making chili, no carne?

VEGETARIAN CHILI

Soupée:

> 1 clove garlic, crushed
>
> 1 medium onion, sliced

in 1 frozen vegetable soup cube (1 minute in the microwave on Medium-High).

Stir into combined:

> 1 can (14 oz/398 mL) kidney beans, drained,[44] and
>
> 1 cup (250 mL) cooked rice

Stir in:

> 1 tbsp (15 mL) chopped jalapeños
>
> 1 green pepper, chopped
>
> ½ cup (125 mL) chopped celery

Add (optional):

> ¼ cup (50 mL) salsa

Before serving, sprinkle with:

> 2 tbsp (25 mL) grated sharp cheese

Even keeping this to a minimum, it's more than one serving. Ladle enough for dinner into your microwave dish and heat it, adding the cheese and zapping again to make it oozy. You'll notice I don't precook the pepper or celery. I like the crunch. If you don't, soupée them along with the garlic and onion.

Leftover Advice:

> Stuff it into a burrito, adding more grated cheese and salsa before heating. Or, smear it all over nachos, top with more cheese and heat it. Chili freezes well, but vary the servings. Add frozen

44 *SPEAKING OF CHILI, WHY LIMIT YOURSELF TO ONE KIND OF BEAN? BECAUSE WITH ONLY ONE PERSON EATING, YOU'LL HAVE TOO MUCH LEFT OVER, THAT'S WHY. I'M GLAD I ASKED.*

corn to one dish, some cooked rice to another, extra jalapeños or salsa to another. Cover with plastic and with foil to keep it from drying out. Even so, you'll do well to add extra salsa when you thaw it.

BAKED POTATO[45]

45 *IN MY OTHER LIFE A BAKED POTATO HAD NO BUSINESS APPEARING IN A LIST OF ENTRÉES. NO MATTER, IT'S DINNER NOW AND IT'S GOOD.*

1 big, beautiful baking potato

Choice of one or more of the following:

1) ½ cup (125 mL) low-fat cottage cheese, mixed with
snipped green onions
lemon–black pepper seasoning

2) grated Jarlsberg cheese (or your choice)
couple of leftover asparagus spears, cut up

3) hot salsa
Mexican cheese spread

4) low-fat yogurt
lumpfish caviar

5) 2 snipped green onions, mixed with
½ cup (125 mL) low-fat sour cream
lots of freshly ground black pepper

6) cooked chopped spinach, mixed with
Feta-Garlic Crumbles (p. 96)

7) tuna fish (see tuna salad filling, p. 131, 132)

8) go on and live a little: load it with butter and salt and pig out![46]

46 *WHAT ELSE ARE YOU GOING TO DO WITH ALL THAT LEFTOVER BUTTER?*

No matter which combination you choose, bake the potato until done. My microwave oven cooks a good-sized potato in 11 to 13 minutes; more powerful ovens take less time, about 4-7 minutes. Split the potato open lengthwise and squish it open to receive guests.

Spoon one of the above mixtures in, over and around the potato and either zap it again or broil it or eat it instantly, depending on the contents and your mood.

Wherever you bake your potato—microwave, toaster-oven, conventional oven—be sure to pierce it in several places with a large-tined fork or small paring knife so it won't explode.

Leftover Advice:

If you can't eat all your potato, save the shell for potato skins (see p. 135). Or bake two potatoes and use the second one for two more meals: put the innards into fish chowder and save the outards for cheesy skins.

SWEET POTATO AND VEG

1 sweet potato, peeled and thickly sliced

3 or 4 parsnips, ditto

10 carrots, scraped and cut into thick pieces

1 whole fennel bulb, cut into appetizing chunks

2 tbsp (25 mL) oil

seasoning to taste

Cut the vegetables into a large casserole and toss them in the oil and seasoning. Roast them, covered, at 350°F (180°C) for 30 minutes or less, stirring a couple of times. These are good on their own as well as with a broiled hamburger, broiled chicken or a grilled turkey patty.

Leftover Advice:

These vegetables ripen into wonderful leftovers and keep for several days. Reheat in the microwave. (And although it's not supposed to be, I have frozen this dish and it's fine.)

The buzz word in current food fashion is fibre. Lots of fibre, we are told, is good for what ails us, aiding elimination, as it is delicately called. We all take cold breakfast cereal so much for granted now, we tend to forget that it is, in fact, fibre. So is bran as in bran muffins. While you're getting used to the idea of introducing more fibre into your diet as well as your soul, here's a bouquet of ideas to give you heart's ease and swift dinners:

° Add some of your cooked brown rice to canned lentils,[47] maybe with curry.
° Spike canned black beans with black bean sauce with garlic. Add chopped green peppers for colour.
° Thin refried beans with a little yogurt, drape it over nachos on a pie plate, add salsa and a small amount of grated sharp Cheddar and heat in the microwave.[48]
° Heat canned pinto beans with chopped olives, red peppers, baby carrots and/or corn niblets, plus salsa and crushed garlic. It's not hard to be vegetarian as long as the taste buds are singing.

47 *DO YOU KNOW THAT HOME-GROWN GREEN LENTILS HAVE TWICE THE FIBRE OF IMPORTED RED?*

48 *SOME PEOPLE WOULD CALL THIS A SNACK BUT IT'S PRETTY LARGE AND LOADED WITH CALORIES.*

° You can stuff just about anything I have mentioned into pita pockets (whole wheat, please). Add chopped fresh romaine and tomatoes for cold lunch, or grated cheese and heat-a-pita for a hot supper.

In my time I have seen the rise and fall of protein, the ascendancy of carbohydrates, the acceptance of pasta and the veneration of broccoli, not to mention root vegetables—all that beautiful beta-carotene! We've come a long way from roast beef, potatoes with gravy and peas.[49] Not far enough, of course.

49 IN MY OTHER LIFE I WENT TO SCOTLAND WITH MY HUSBAND AND STOPPED AT A COUNTRY HOTEL OUTSIDE OF GLASGOW WHERE WE HAD DINNER: BEEF ROASTED SO LONG IT WAS GREY, POTATOES BOILED SO LONG THEY WERE FLAKING APART, PEAS COOKED SO LONG THEY WERE DRIED UP AND DIMPLED. WHILE I WAS LOOKING WITH DISMAY AT THE FOOD ON MY PLATE, BILL STARTED TO LAUGH. HE LAUGHED SO HARD THE TEARS WERE COMING OUT OF HIS EYES.

"WHAT'S SO FUNNY?" I ASKED.

"OH," HE SAID, SIGHING AND WIPING HIS EYES. "IT'S JUST LIKE MOTHER USED TO COOK."

CHAPTER NINE

Company:
Guests, Children, Lovers and Others

Laughter is good relish for a meal, whether it's company or family.

~ Betty Jane Wylie

Sooner or later, every single person has to break down and invite someone to break bread, if not share a meal. It's a good idea to have company as often as is comfortable and affordable because that's the only way the living room gets picked up and the bathroom cleaned. Company makes good house-keepers of us all.[1]

Once we have the ground rules established—the guest (whether occasional, special or spasmodically live-in), environment fairly clean and presentable—the question remains: What will you have for dinner? And what will you do with the leftovers all by yourself?

Chicken is always a safe thing to serve company. I know a single who serves chicken every time she has me for dinner. She doesn't remember and I

1 MOST PEOPLE CAN LIVE WITH THEIR OWN SQUALOR FOR LONGER THAN IS READILY BELIEVED.

don't mind, because she fixes it quite differently every time—one breast each, and no leftovers. She does a nice thing with green grapes.[2] On the other hand, here is a single's chance to cook a roast or a turkey. Big meat is a good choice if you're still carnivorous. Singles rarely cook large pieces of meat for themselves. Having company gives them the opportunity to use their teeth and the leftovers are easy.

I'm a "there" cook. I don't mind making an effort in the kitchen and my food tastes pretty good, but I don't present it well. I just say, "There!" and let people take it or leave it. I have a single friend who festoons everything artistically with parsley. It looks so pretty you think she's gone to a lot of trouble even when she hasn't. I like to *eat* parsley, not decorate with it. I have another friend who has no luck with desserts: they always break coming out of the pan (cake) or crumble (pastry) or dribble around the edges (chilled or jelled things). She gets around this by always having whipped cream on hand (the real kind, in a can). When dessert looks messy, she covers it with whipped cream and if anyone asks what it is, she says, "Dieter's Delight," meaning, don't ask, and no one does because if you can't break your diet when you're out for dinner, when can you?

I'll give you a couple of "There!" dinners for company and then we'll negotiate custody.

2 GREEN GRAPES ALWAYS MAKE A COOK LOOK THOUGHTFUL, AS THOUGH SPECIAL CARE HAS BEEN TAKEN AND ATTENTION PAID.

COMPANY FISH FOR SIX OR EIGHT

1 whole (or a very large piece of) fresh salmon or halibut, about 4 lb (2 kg)

1 tsp (5 mL) dried dill

1 lemon, thinly sliced

½ cup (125 mL) dry white wine

Lay the fish out on a piece of foil large enough to wrap around it. Wipe the cavity thoroughly and then put a layer of lemon slices into it. Sprinkle dill over the lemon. Pull the edges of the foil up around the fish, but before you seal it, pour the wine over it. Drugstore wrap and place the package in a roasting pan. Bake it (really, it's oven-poaching) at 400°F (200°C) for 30 to 45 minutes. (The rule is 10 minutes per inch thickness of the fish.) Serve on a platter, garnished with parsley if you wish. Carve with a fish knife and fork, peeling off the skin and lifting delectable chunks off the bones. Eat it with obscene amounts of aioli[3] or Hollandaise, plus hot new potatoes and asparagus, cold cherry tomatoes and cold cooked shrimp, warm French bread, lots of white wine.

Leftovers are welcome. The fish is delicious cold with more of that sauce or mayo.

3 IF YOU DARE.

COMPANY BEEF FOR SIX OR EIGHT

How about a hunk of meat?

> 1 eye-of-round roast, 4–5 lb (2 kg)
>
> garlic clove
>
> salad oil
>
> dry mustard
>
> freshly ground black pepper

Allow the meat to come to room temperature. Rub it with the cut garlic clove and then massage it lightly with a handful of salad oil. Mix the seasonings and rub them all around the meat. Set the oven at 400°F (200°C) and put the meat in. When the oven hits that temperature turn it down to 325°F (160°C) and cook the meat for about an hour (15–20 minutes per pound.) If you use a meat thermometer, just bring it to rare (about 140°F/60°C). Treat it like steak and serve with a Caesar salad, fresh asparagus, tiny boiled new potatoes, etc.

Leftover Advice:

> Serve leftover strips of meat with aioli, or in a stir-fry. It's so lovely and rare, you can get away with an open-face steak sandwich: lots of garlic butter spread on thick slices of toasted French bread, and the meat. If you must, you can heat it quickly in the microwave, but you run the risk of it not being as rare and tasting like a boarding-house special.

COMPANY TURKEY FOR FOUR TO SIX

> 1 turkey breast
>
> 1 cup (250 mL) red wine
>
> ¼ cup (50 mL) olive oil
>
> freshly ground black pepper
>
> 1 tsp (5 mL) dried rosemary, crushed

Put the turkey breast in a shallow dish just large enough to hold it. Mix the remaining ingredients and pour the marinade over the meat, turning once. Cover and refrigerate for several hours (or all day), turning a couple of times. Broil or barbecue at least 6 inches (15 cm) from the heat, basting with the marinade and turning frequently, for at least an hour or until a meat thermometer inserted into center of the breast measures 185°F (85°C). Check it for doneness; the meat should be white, not pink. This is wonderful with grilled vegetables, wild rice or sweet potatoes—but no marshmallows, please!

Leftover Advice:

> My current favourite leftover turkey is turkey fajitas (p. 101).

I used to date a twice-divorced man who owned two forks.[4] When he found out I could cook he asked me to cook dinner for a bunch of friends he owed. That was no challenge until I took stock of his equipment. Long before medieval dinners became the in-thing for tourists[5] I cooked and served one to my friend's guests. I used the two forks for servers to spear the vegetables. A sharp knife was shared for those who needed it. Lots of paper napkins and, at the end of the meal, one big finger bowl took care of the greasy fingers. He had enough wine glasses. Here's the menu:

4 *THAT'S THE DIFFERENCE BETWEEN DIVORCE AND WIDOWHOOD. A BEREAVED PERSON ENDS UP WITH ALL THE FORKS. NOT AS MUCH COMPENSATION AS YOU MIGHT THINK.*

5 *LOOSE IN THE COURT OF HENRY IV, A MEDIEVAL ROMP.*

A FORKLESS DINNER FOR DIVORCÉS

loin lamb chops, broiled

chicken drumsticks, broiled

whole roasted potatoes and carrots

a whole loaf of crusty bread, warmed

choice of several mustards

cherry tomatoes and celery sticks

fresh fruit in season, to be eaten out of hand

The amount you cook depends on the number of guests you have. This is finger food at its very best, an easy meal to prepare and serve, and by the time it's over, everyone is very greasy and friendly.

CUSTODY

One of the fringe benefits of being handed back your life is being awarded custody of yourself.

~ *Merle Shain*

You know that old line about your children being guests in your house so be polite? At no time is this more valid than when you have joint custody. Besides being polite to your kids, you have to feed them. Being a part-time parent, with a child or children who live in according to regularly scheduled arrangements, may mean that lots of singles have custody for dinner several times a week. That means they have to plan and cook for more than one some of the time and cope with leftovers most of the time.[6]

I'm assuming your custodial guests are fairly young with the young, fresh (picky) palates of the young.[7] They like simple food, not too spicy, and most of them prefer things not to touch each other on the plate, so casseroles are out, except for the first recipe I suggest. The beauty of most of the food I suggest is that leftovers are implicit and simple. They also bear repetition, which children like. In a world that has changed so drastically for them, why not let them count on food?

6 PERHAPS THIS PROBLEM GIVES US ANOTHER REASON FOR THE POPULARITY OF STIR-FRIES. GIVE ME A DELIGHTFUL MIXTURE OF TENDER-COOKED VEGETABLES AND MEASURED PASTA (IT PAYS TO GET A PASTA MEASURER), AND I'LL SHOW YOU A MEAL FOR A PART-TIME FAMILY WITH NO AFTERMATH.

7 WHEN YOU'VE LIVED AS LONG AS I HAVE, AND HAVE A LONG MEMORY, YOU'LL FIND YOU REMEMBER NOT ONLY YOUR CHILDREN'S FOOD LIKES, DISLIKES, FOIBLES AND PREJUDICES BUT ALSO YOUR GRANDCHILDREN'S. OVER THE YEARS I'VE DEVELOPED A FEW TRICKS TO SATISFY EVERY-ONE—IF NOT ALL THE TIME, AT LEAST SOME OF IT.

You'll immediately notice something about the following recipe: I'm not counting fat grams. Kids need fat. They don't need junk but they need fat. You'll also notice this isn't Kraft Dinner.

CUSTODIAL MACARONI

1 cup (250 mL) elbow macaroni

2 tbsp (25 mL) butter

2 tbsp (25 mL) flour

2 cups (500 mL) milk, heated

1 egg, beaten

salt and freshly ground black pepper to taste

½ tsp (2 mL) dry mustard

½ tsp (2 mL) Worcestershire sauce

½ cup (125 mL) dry white wine

2 cups (500 mL) grated Cheddar cheese

½ cup (125 mL) dry bread crumbs

Boil the macaroni, rinse in cold water, drain well, and transfer to a buttered 1½-quart casserole. In a saucepan, melt the butter over medium heat, stir in the flour to make a roux, and cook stirring, for a minute. Whisk in the hot milk and cook, stirring, until thickened. Add the egg, seasonings and wine, and heat through but don't let it curdle. Reduce the heat to low and stir in 1½ cups (375 mL) of the cheese in small amounts, letting the cheese melt but not allowing the sauce to boil. When the cheese

has melted in, combine the sauce with the macaroni in the baking dish. Toss the remaining cheese
with the bread crumbs and strew over the surface.
Bake at 400°F (200°C) for 25 to 30 minutes. Serves
4. How about toast and sliced tomatoes with it?

A taco platter solves a number of problems when
you have children as your guests. They get to pick
and choose from an array of foods and can avoid
what they don't like without anyone fussing at
them. The only rule is that they must eat what they
assemble.

CUSTODIAL TACOS

    1 lb (500 g) lean ground beef

    1 taco sauce mix

    a choice of the following, in separate
    bowls:
    sliced avocado
    chopped tomatoes
    shredded lettuce
    grated Cheddar or Monterey Jack cheese
    thinly sliced green peppers
    salsa
    refried beans
    taco shells

Prepare the ground beef according to the directions
on the package of taco sauce mix. Chop, slice, grate
and arrange the remaining ingredients in serving
bowls on the dining table. Warm the taco shells and
let the kids have their way with the food.

    As for the leftovers, see p. 101.

Children are often not big meat eaters, for which these days you can be grateful. However, if you want to teach them about meat, a beef fondue is a great way to start. It worked with one of my kids when he was four and he has never looked back. Do you still have a fondue pot? (Did you ever have one?)

If you don't, you can use an electric fry pan with a long cord to heat the oil at the table. Be very careful, but then you have to be careful with hot oil no matter how you heat it. A friend of mine blew up the centrepiece when she tried to refill and relight her fondue pot at the table. Don't do that.

CUSTODIAL BEEF FONDUE

4 cups (1 L) peanut oil

lean (expensive) beef (4 oz/125 g per person)

various sauces, to your taste

Use peanut oil for your fondue pot as it seems to me to have the least smell and the lowest flammability. Provide everyone with plates and fondue forks and the rules: If you drop a piece of meat in the oil, you have to kiss the person on your left. (This makes children very careful, to avoid kissing a sibling or a parent at table.) Everyone cooks, choosing the amount and the desired temperature of the meat to be consumed, and dipping it in the sauce of choice. Choices can include:

hot mustard

horseradish

Béarnaise sauce (bottled?)

ketchup

aïoli (?)

dare I say—Szechuan?

Here's another fondue I resurrected recently to accommodate one of my young families with a vegetarian in its midst. It's another meal that appeals to young and old.

CUSTODIAL CHEESE FONDUE

2 cups (500 mL) dry white wine[8]

a small splash of vinegar (to help keep the cheese from separating)

7–8 cups (1.75-2 L) grated cheese (Emmenthal, Gruyère, Cheddar)

1 or 2 handfuls of all-purpose flour

½ tsp (2 mL) dry mustard, sprinkled over the cheese

8 I CONSULTED WITH THE FATHER ABOUT THIS, HAVING READY, IN CASE HE DISAPPROVED OF THE WINE, CANNED CHEESE SOUP. HOWEVER, HE KNEW THAT THE ALCOHOL EVAPORATES AND OPTED FOR THE WINE.

Dipping things:

Besides offering a basket of crusty bread torn into swirl-size pieces, fill a platter with an attractive arrangement of cauliflowerets, broccoli flowers, cherry tomatoes, mushrooms, chunks of green and red pepper, Belgian endive leaves, and for the flesh eaters, cooked cocktail shrimp, thick pepperoni slices, cubes of canned ham or luncheon meat, or canned cocktail franks.

Heat the wine gently on the stove, adding the vinegar. When it's at melting temperature, add the grated cheese a handful at a time, and stir it in. To help the cheese keep its aplomb, and also to thicken the sauce, toss it with a handful or two of flour after it's grated and before you stir it into the wine.

This should be a thick sauce, one you can swirl the food around in and glop up to your mouth, napkins at the ready. Kids love it. The best news is that it's an easy way to persuade kids to eat their vegetables. This do-it-yourself stuff can get to be a habit. It's an easy formula for feeding children; they eat better when they have some control and choice.

Leftover Advice:
> Any leftover fondue sauce can be poured over your next pasta or vegetables, or spread over a pizza round.

CUSTODIAL PIZZAS

individual pizza rounds, ready to bake

a selection of:
grated Mozzarella or Cheddar cheese
grated Parmesan cheese
chopped tomatoes
chopped green peppers
pepperoni slices
pizza or pasta sauce
Feta-Garlic Crumbles (p. 96)
crisp bacon
anchovies

You can put anything you or the children like on their pizzas, as much or as little as you have available. They each build their own pizzas, the rule being they must eat what they concoct. You bake it for them (according to the directions on the pizza round package) and they eat it. Division of labour, and spoils.

The nicest thing about these meals is their easy, no-pressure style, easy for the cook to prepare, easy for the child to eat, and no pressure on either side if they're feeling a little awkward after being apart awhile. Single some-time parents appreciate that.

Don't forget all the lovely stir-fries you can make. Most kids love pasta, and you can sneak a few more vegetables in with it when they're not looking.

Not to forget a little exploration. My granddaughter Meg told me how to handle the Parchment Pillows. Maybe a child you know will teach you something new to put in the package.

Pillow talk comes next.

SEX

What do great sex and great foods have in common? Each makes you ravenous for more.

~ *Gael Greene*

Smoked salmon comes to mind in this context, but it's expensive. Try *gravad lax*, a very sexy food, even better than smoked, and a little cheaper.

GRAVAD LAX[9]

1 tbsp (5 mL) sugar

2 tbsp (25 mL) or less salt

1 tsp (5 mL) black peppercorns

9 MY COUSIN HERBORG IN REYKJAVIK GAVE ME THIS RECIPE.

1 bunch fresh dill OR ½ to 1 cup
(125 to 250 mL) dried dill

1 lb (500 g) salmon fillets in 2 pieces,
skin on, deboned

½ tsp (2 mL) lemon juice, if required

Grind the pepper and mix it with the salt and sugar.
Lay out a large sheet of foil considerably bigger
than a salmon fillet. Lay down a thick bed of dill the
same size as a fillet, then sprinkle it with the seasoning mixture. Place the first fillet skin side down
on this prepared area, then do another number (dill
and seasonings) on the upside of this fish. Lay the
other fillet on top, skin side up, head-to-toe, i.e.
opposite, so they sort of match in shape and come
out an even thickness.

More seasonings on that and then another thick
layer of dill. If you feel like it, put ½ tsp (2 mL) of
lemon juice in the foil package before you seal it
tightly with a drugstore wrap. (I usually wait until
the first time I open it, before I bother with the
lemon juice.)

Put the package in a pan with sides, place a
weight on it, not too heavy, just enough to encourage it to sweat, and store it in the fridge. After
24 hours, turn the package over. If it has leaked,
your package was not sealed tightly enough; save
the juice, and pour it on the fish when you open
the package.

After 24 hours, turn again. This amount of fish
will probably be ready to eat after 48 hours; it should
be uniformly pickled, and look like a moist smoked
salmon. If it's not, give it another 12. It will keep 7 to
10 days in the fridge, well sealed (add more lemon
juice if it needs moistening), and 6 months in the

freezer. Mine gets eaten within five days, so I've never had a problem with storage. Serve with French bread or a good brown bread and Mustard-Dill Sauce.

MUSTARD-DILL SAUCE

¼ cup (50 mL) Dijon mustard

¼ cup (50 mL) honey mustard OR more Dijon, mixed with 1 tsp (5 mL) sugar

a few drops of olive oil

a bunch of fresh dill

Work this out in your mini-processor. If you don't have one, then mix the sugar and dill into Dijon mustard with enough oil to bring it to an easy spreading consistency.

I know, I know, this is a cookbook for singles, but as I have pointed out, even singles entertain sometimes and where better, on certain occasions, than in bed? While food and sex have much in common,[10] there are some interesting differences. For example, people discuss food and exchange favourite recipes much more openly and frequently than they reveal any new or effective techniques of sex.

All this by way of introduction to a significant use of food by singles in bed, that is, fork play. Consistent with the taboos of our time, I will not attempt any advice or creative suggestions regarding your activities in bed. The only eating I will discuss is that of food. I will limit myself to before and after discussions and not during. Although like most people I am at heart a voyeur and would love to watch and make suggestions, I won't spoil your fun; some

10 *I MYSELF, BEING A GIFTED AMATEUR IN BOTH FIELDS, HAVE RECOMMENDED AND DESCRIBED THE TOPICAL APPLICATION OF CHAMPAGNE, BEING A RELATED ELEMENT, BUT I HAVE NEVER DONE SO FOR MONEY OR IN PRINT.*

discoveries are best made for oneself and in the heat of the moment, as it were, and at one's own speed and level of tolerance.

"I've always had a voyeur's interest in eating on the sly," writes Maggie Waldron in her imaginative cookbook, *Cold Spaghetti at Midnight*. Before you jump to the conclusion that she's talking about après-sex food, let me say that the book is more like folk medicine than sex counsel. Waldron considers food as front-line treatment for what ails you, not for what it can do for you in the bedroom when you're not sick.

Of course, I conducted a survey among single friends to find out what kind of dinner they served to someone they expected to have around for breakfast.[11]

I like to cater to the aggressive instinct in a man by offering flank steak.[12] Flank steak tastes good and the leftovers are wonderful for a picnic later—in bed? Hang the expense.

LONDON BROIL

1 cup (250 mL) red wine

½ cup (125 mL) olive oil

1 clove garlic, crushed

salt

freshly ground black pepper

1 flank steak

In the morning make a marinade of the wine, oil, garlic, salt and pepper and pour it over the meat in a dish large enough to hold it spread out flat. Let it steep all day, covered, in the fridge and turn it a

11 MY MOST MEMORABLE INTER-VIEW WAS WITH A YOUNG MAN, OBVIOUSLY GIFTED AT COOKING AS WELL AS OTHER THINGS, WHO WENT SO FAR AS TO DESCRIBE FOR ME A WEEK OF MENUS, A DIFFERENT ONE FOR EVERY NIGHT, THOUGH THE WOMAN WAS ALSO DIFFERENT EVERY NIGHT AND WOULDN'T HAVE KNOWN IF IT WAS A REPEAT. HE DIDN'T WANT TO GET BORED, HE SAID. I COULD TELL. BUT HE SAID HE'D NEVER DO IT AGAIN. HIS CHIEF MEMORY OF THE WEEK WAS THE WASHING UP.

12 IN MY OTHER LIFE I DISCOVERED THIS MEAT UNDER THE TITLE LONDON BROIL WHEN FOOD WRITERS WERE TRYING TO CONVINCE CONSUMERS THAT IT WAS WORTH THE TROUBLE. IT IS, BUT IT'S ALMOST NOT WORTH THE PRICE THESE DAYS. IT USED TO BE A BARGAIN BUT NOW IT'S PRICED UP THERE WITH THE MORE TENDER CUTS LIKE T-BONE AND NEW YORK STRIP.

couple of times, before you leave for work and when you get home. Bring it to room temperature before you cook it. Broil it 3 inches from the heat for about 3 to 4 minutes a side, depending how thick it is. You want the meat seared and brown on the outside and rare but hot within—that's why you had it at room temperature, so it would give in.

To serve, cut the entire steak in thin slices across the diagonal. Wrap any leftover slices in foil and store in the fridge; it won't last long.

This is a classic meal, not to say a cliché, so go ahead and serve it with baked potatoes, a Caesar salad and a bottle of good red wine. Dessert comes later.

CAESAR SALAD

romaine lettuce, torn into bite-sized pieces

4 cloves garlic (or none, depending on your guest)

1 tin anchovy fillets, oil included

3 tbsp (45 mL) lemon juice

a splash of Worcestershire sauce

olive oil as necessary

freshly ground black pepper

freshly grated Parmesan cheese

chapons[13]

Tear the romaine into a bowl, cover it with paper towelling and let it wait in the fridge for you. To make the dressing, using your mini-processor or not, first smush the garlic, then add the anchovies

13 *NOW, ABOUT CHAPONS. I KNOW YOU DON'T WANT TO SPEND MUCH TIME IN THE KITCHEN BUT YOU REALLY WILL SAVE TIME AND MONEY IF YOU MAKE YOUR OWN. LET'S BE CLEAR ABOUT THIS: CROUTONS ARE USUALLY SMALL CUBES OF BREAD THAT HAVE BEEN LIGHTLY SAUTÉED IN OIL UNTIL CRISP, USED FOR TOSSING INTO SALADS AND ON TOP OF SOUP. THEY CAN ALSO BE LARGE, THE SIZE OF A TRIMMED THICK SLICE OF BREAD, FOR LAYING UNDER A CORNISH GAME HEN. THEY DO NOT KEEP.*

CHAPONS, ON THE OTHER HAND, ARE DRY AND KEEP FOR-EVER UNLESS YOUR SON COMES TO VISIT AND FINDS THE TIN THEY'RE IN AND EATS THEM LIKE PEANUTS. TAKE A LOAF OF RYE BREAD AND CUT IT INTO CUBES, NOT BOTHERING TO REMOVE THE CRUSTS. THROW THE CUBES IN A LARGE ROASTING PAN, TOSS THEM WITH A GENEROUS BLIZZARD OF GARLIC SALT AND TOAST THEM AT 325°F (160°C) FOR AN HOUR OR SO, STIRRING EVERY ONCE IN A WHILE, UNTIL THEY ARE GOLDEN AND VERY CRISP.

and their oil and blend them with the lemon juice and Wooster. With the motor running, add the olive oil until you get a nice emulsion—that's a scientific word for dressing. When you're ready to serve the salad, toss it gently with the dressing.[14] Grind the pepper over it, sprinkle the Parmesan cheese and toss again. Strew the chapons and toss once more; if they don't show up enough, scatter some more on the surface.

I haven't mentioned dessert. Personally, I think there is no occasion that cannot be enhanced by champagne. A perfect dessert for this meal would be fresh strawberries and champagne. Wash, drain on paper towels, but do not hull the strawberries; you need the handles. Dip or soak them one by one in a flute of champagne and feed each other.

If you want more than that, make a chocolate dip and do what comes naturally. If price is no object, buy a package of Toblerone chocolate and melt it with a little evaporated milk as moisturizer. You could also add a drop or two of Kahlua or brandy. When you've stirred and blended it to the desired consistency, pour it into a little fondue pot with a votary candle underneath it and offer a prayer of thanks for chocolate and other blessings.

Here's a less expensive way of gilding your strawberry.

14 LOOK, MAW, NO EGG!

CHOCOLATE DIP

    3 oz (85 g) semi-sweet chocolate

    2 tsp (10 mL) butter

    evaporated milk

    liqueur to taste (optional)

Melt the chocolate and butter in a double boiler over hot water, or zap it in a little microwave dish on Medium heat, taking it out a couple of times to stir and melt the chocolate. Add the evaporated milk and liqueur to bring it to dipping consistency. Use as a dip for other fruit besides strawberries and don't forget the champagne.

If you want to make a little more impressive but easy fuss, try this:

PEARS AMARETTO

> 1 Anjou pear per person
>
> 1 cup (250 mL) simple syrup[15]
>
> 1 tbsp (15 mL) Amaretto per pear
>
> 2 tbsp (25 mL) almond cookie crumbs per pear
>
> Poire William liqueur (optional)

15 TO MAKE SIMPLE SYRUP, STIR
    2 TSP (10 ML) OF SUGAR INTO
    1 CUP (250 ML) WATER AND HEAT
    IN THE MICROWAVE TO DISSOLVE.
    STIR AGAIN AND USE.

Peel the pears and cut a slice off the bottom of each to make it stand firmly upright. Place the pears in a deep oven-proof dish, pour the syrup in to a depth of 1 inch (2.5 cm) and spoon over each pear 1 tbsp (15 mL) Amaretto. Bake for 30 minutes at 350°F (180°C), basting a couple of times. Remove from oven and sprinkle each pear with cookie crumbs. Serve in individual bowls and pass the Poire William *eau de vie* for embellishment at will.

If you peel the pears ahead of time, put them in cold water to cover to keep them from going brown.

I still remember the first bottle of kirsch I ever bought. This potent, high-proof, cherry-flavoured *eau de vie* was all the rage for a while and I was trying it out on everything, stirring it into cheese fondue, pouring it into fruit compotes, setting it alight in Cherries Jubilee.

The simplest, best way to savour it was in whipped cream, added instead of vanilla in the final folding. I suggest lacing your whipped cream with kirsch if you want a smash ending to an evening. Into every single's life a little fun must fall.[16]

As for breakfast, you made dinner. I think it's only fair if you were served breakfast in bed.

16 WE HAD CLOSE FRIENDS FOR DINNER ONE EVENING AND I SERVED A GORGEOUS FRESH FRUIT PLATTER WITH AN ENORMOUS MOUND OF WHIPPED CREAM TO LAVISH ON IT.

MY FRIEND'S HUSBAND WAS A STAID, CONSERVATIVE MAN AS BEFITTED A YOUNG LAWYER. AS FAR AS I KNEW, HE HAD NO WEAKNESSES. HE NEVER DRANK TO EXCESS, HE DIDN'T SMOKE, HE WATCHED HIS DIET, HE LOVED HIS WIFE (STILL DOES). HE ALSO LOVED WHIPPED CREAM. AFTER HIS THIRD HELPING HE VOLUNTEERED A THOUGHT THAT SURPRISED ME.

"KNOW WHAT I'D LIKE TO DO WITH THIS WHIPPED CREAM?" HE ASKED US IMPETUOUSLY, WITHOUT WAITING FOR A REPLY. "SPREAD IT ALL OVER NANCIE AND LICK IT OFF."

CHAPTER TEN

Are You Having Fun Yet?

*Research tells us that fourteen out of any
ten individuals like chocolate.*

~ *Sarah Boynton*

*F*un is like comfort food: difficult to define and different for everyone, as unique and individual as you are. Fun is closely related to your morale and to your self-image, and you're the most likely person to supply all three. Not that I'm recommending blatant and conspicuous consumption or health-damaging over-indulgence. The point of this whole book has been to be good to yourself in a healthy way. That means buying and eating what you like, of course, not only enough food but the proper foods. Treat your body to a decent set of vitamins and minerals. Bear in mind, however, that we don't live by bread alone; sometimes we need cake—within reason.

An angel food cake, made from your accumulation of egg whites in the freezer and according to your favourite recipe or made from a mix (easy and incredibly lofty!), is the lightest low-fat, most delicious cake you can indulge in, and fun with a chocolate fondue and lots of fresh fruit as well. Chocolate is fun for most people.

Sometimes fun is blander than chocolate and synonymous with comfort. Here's a vanilla comfort to make you feel cherished.

COMFORTING CUSTARD

1 egg

pinch of salt

1 tbsp (15 mL) vanilla sugar OR ½ tsp (2 mL) vanilla extract

1 tbsp (15 mL) sugar

1 cup (250 mL) whole milk

nutmeg

Beat the egg with the salt, then stir in the vanilla, sugar and the milk. Pour into two small oven-proof buttered custard dishes. Set them in a pan of hot water, about an inch deep, but not so deep as to float them. Grate a little nutmeg over the custards before you bake them at 350°F (180°C) for 30 to 35 minutes. They're done when a knife pushed into the centre comes out clean. Makes 2 very small servings. You'll probably eat them both in one sitting.

Candy is dandy, too, not necessarily chocolate, and you can make your own if you need a fix at midnight.

COMFORTING PEANUT BRITTLE

1 cup (250 mL) sugar

¼ tsp (4 mL) salt

1 cup (250 mL) peanuts

Butter a foil pie pan and set it aside. Heat the sugar and salt in a heavy saucepan over medium-high heat, stirring it steadily with a wooden spoon until it melts and then caramelizes; this takes only 2 or 3 minutes, so don't leave it alone. When it happens, stir in the peanuts—fast!—and pour the mixture into the pie pan before it hardens in the pot. Break it up when it's cool and smash into it.

Listen, I know this is supposed to be a cookbook, but I've broken so many rules already and I'm almost finished, so bear with me. I'm talking about food and the single person, so everything you do with food, in or out of the kitchen, is relevant, and that includes eating out.

Singles do. Eat. Out. A recent survey revealed that people eating alone now account for more than 20 per cent of restaurant clientele. Not only do singles get tired of their own cooking, and yes, of take-out too, and want to be served a good dinner they had nothing to do with preparing, they also have to eat when they're working. Sooner or later most businesspeople, single or not, male or female, have to go out of town for their work. They have to eat out in alien cities, but not only alien. A late night at the office, a hard day one doesn't want to make harder by cooking, a need to be treated well (comforted), all these reasons can send a single to a "nice place to eat," that is, one with tablecloths and napkins, a waiter and a wine list. So restaurateurs and waiters had better be nice to that solitary diner they stuck by the kitchen door; today's solo may be tomorrow's office party.

If they do stick you by the kitchen door, try politely to suggest you'd like to sit somewhere else. If you had a reservation, and if the place isn't crowded, you're entitled. I like to sit with my back to a wall; corners are even better. So if a waiter tries to stick me in the middle of the room or, worse, by a pillar but with no wall at my back, I ask for a different table. Often you don't want to make a fuss, but if you intend to enjoy your meal and make it special, take the time to explain to the waiter what you want: a good meal. Discuss the menu, confer about the wine, be friendly. Waiters have noticed that a single will often spend more for a solitary dinner than one diner does in the company of others.[1]

Hotel dining rooms are the best bets for singles, probably because there are so many solitary transients. I have had some of the best meals and the best service in hotels.[2] I have had *lagniappe*[3] offered me by a sympathetic maitre d'hotel, an attentive waiter, an admiring sommelier, even a grateful chef in return for my appreciation. That unsolicited, free bonus has usually taken the form of a cognac or liqueur with my coffee tendered as a compliment to my good taste. It's like a reward for good behaviour and adds to the fun of an evening out.

You know the line about stopping to sniff the flowers,[4] meaning you should enjoy yourself going by on the way to somewhere. The flowers don't have to be hothouse, but sometimes they can and ought to be. Say you're out of town, perhaps on a weekend conference, or a five-day workathon. Granted, you're out most of the day, but you also have home-

1 DON'T FORGET TO TIP WELL AND GIVE ALL US SINGLES A GOOD REPUTATION.

2 HERE'S AN UNADVERTISED SERVICE I LEARNED ABOUT FROM A SYMPATHETIC WAITER. IF YOU ARE A GUEST IN THE HOTEL AND YOU ORDER A WHOLE BOTTLE OF WINE WITH YOUR DINNER THAT YOU CAN'T POSSIBLY FINISH, THE DINING ROOM WILL HAVE THE OPENED BOTTLE DELIVERED TO YOUR ROOM.

3 *LAGNIAPPE* IS A CREOLE WORD, FROM *LA*, FRENCH FOR *THE*, AND *NAPA*, A SPANISH VARIATION OF *YAPA*, MEANING A PRESENT TO A CUSTOMER. THE WAY I HEARD IT WAS THAT THE MERCHANTS OF

work to do at night and you are stuck in a bare room in a strange city with a bunch of strangers. Go to the hotel florist and buy yourself a flower. It often need only be one: alstremeria and freesia have several blooms on one stem. If I haven't had the foresight to take a small bud vase with me,[5] then I buy an inexpensive one.

I also travel with either a hot pot or an immersion heater (depending on the voltage) and a couple of nesting plastic cups. In a small zipped bag I carry powdered milk (I hate artificial creamer) for my tea, tea bags, hot chocolate, decaf cappuccino mix, herbal tea bags, soup packets, a spoon and a small knife. This kit contributes to the pleasure of single travel: the pleasure of morning tea, hotter and earlier than any room service can manage; an inexpensive restful lunch, adding crackers and cheese (from the plane?) to the cuppa-soup, and a delicious unwinding in bed with the hot drink of my choice.

Treating oneself to private moments of luxury is fun. Singles should learn to cultivate such a habit. That's why you toast yourself with a glass of wine at dinner, buy tiny airline-size bottles of Irish Cream to slip a tablespoon into your after-dinner coffee (not every night), occasionally dip your delicious strawberries in your own private well of chocolate (chocolate chips melted in the microwave), and sometimes put real sour cream on your baked potato.

Man does not live by bread alone—no, nor woman either. Sometimes people, human that they are, need to have a little fun. I said a *little*. You're not really living to eat, although no one said you can't enjoy both. What you are doing is eating well, in order to live a healthier life. Be grateful. Be happy. You really are the head honcho.

NEW ORLEANS MADE A HABIT OF GIVING THEIR BEST CUSTOMERS EXTRA LITTLE GOODIES, TO THANK THEM FOR THEIR TRADE.

4 I THINK ARNOLD PALMER SAID IT FIRST, OR MAYBE SOME ANCIENT ROMAN.

5 HONESTLY! I TRAVEL LIGHT, BUT IF I'M SPENDING MORE THAN THREE OR FOUR DAYS, I PLAN ON BUYING A FLOWER AND I HAVE TAKEN MY OWN BUD VASE.

Bibliography

Atwood, Margaret, ed. *The CanLit Foodbook*, A Totem Book, Toronto, 1987.

The Beardstown Ladies Investment Club, with Leslie Whitaker, *The Beardstown Ladies' Common-Sense Investment Guide*, Hyperion, New York, 1994.

Bracken, Peg, *Appendix to The I Hate to Cook Cookbook*, Fawcett, World Library, New York, 1967.

Brillat-Savarin, *Physiologie du Goût*, 1825.

Colwin, Laurie, *Home Cooking: A Writer in the Kitchen*, Alfred A. Knopf, New York, 1988.

de Pomiane, Edouard, translated from the French by Peggie Benton, *Cooking in Ten Minutes or The Adaptation to the Rhythm of Our Time*, Hodder & Stoughton, Australia, 1993.

Dickson, Paul, *The Official Rules*, Delacorte Press, New York, 1978.

___, *The Official Explanations*, Delacorte Press, New York, 1980.

Edwards, John, *The Roman Cookery of Apicius: A Treasury of Gourmet Recipes and Herbal Cookery translated and adapted for the modern kitchen*, Hartley & Marks, Vancouver, B.C., 1984.

Gilbreth, Lillian, Orpha Mae Thomas and Eleanor Clymer, *Management in the Home*, Dodd, Mead & Company, New York, 1959.

Hosford, Mary, *The Missouri Traveller Cookbook*, Farrar Staus & Cudahy, New York, 1958, Ambassador Books, Toronto, 1958.

Huss, Juli I., *The faux Gourmet: A Single Woman's Confession on Food and Sex*, A Dutton Book, Penguin Books, New York, 1994.

Kreschollek, Margie, *The Guaranteed Goof-Proof Healthy Microwave Cookbook*, Bantam Books, New York, Toronto, 1990.

Lindsay, Anne, *Anne Lindsay's Light Kitchen*, Macmillan Canada, Toronto, 1994.

Robbins, Maria Polushkin, *The Cook's Quotation Book: A Literary Feast*, The Pushcart Press, New York, 1983.

Sass, Lorna J., *To the King's Taste: Richard II's book of feasts and recipes adapted for modern cooking*, The Metropolitan Museum of Art, 1975.

Thoreau, Henry David, *Walden*, 1854.

Waldron, Maggie, *Cold Spaghetti at Midnight*, William Morrow and Company, Inc., New York, 1992.

Wylie, Betty Jane, Encore: *The Leftovers Cookbook*, McClelland and Stewart, Toronto, 1979.

Index